Focus on
Careers

A Reference Handbook

TEENAGE PERSPECTIVES

Focus on
Careers

A Reference Handbook

Lynne B. Iglitzin
University of Washington

ABC-CLIO

Santa Barbara, California
Denver, Colorado
Oxford, England

Library of Congress Cataloging-in-Publication Data

Iglitzin, Lynne B., 1931–
    Focus on careers : a reference handbook / Lynne B. Iglitzin.
      p. cm—(Teenage perspectives)
    Includes bibliographical references and index.
    Summary: A guide for young people in choosing educational tracks
and preparing for future careers.
    1. Vocational guidance. 2. Career development. [1. Vocational
guidance.] I. Title. II. Series
    HF5381.I36   1990   650.14–dc20   91-31047

ISBN 0-87436-588-0 (alk.paper)

98 97 96 95 94 93 92 91   10 9 8 7 6 5 4 3 2 1

ABC-CLIO, Inc.
130 Cremona Drive, P.O. Box 1911
Santa Barbara, California 93116-1911

This book is printed on acid-free paper ⊗ .
Manufactured in the United States of America

To Walter

Contents

Chapter 1: You and the World of Work: Life beyond High School, 1

Resources for Finding Out about You and the World of Work, 11

Chapter 2: Understanding Careers: Looking within You, 17

Chapter 6: Nontraditional Career Preparation, 89

Chapter 7: Practical Tips on Career Exploration, 107

Foreword

An old Chinese curse goes, "May you live in exciting times." Today's young people have grown up under such a curse—or blessing. They live in a world that is undergoing dramatic changes on every level—social, political, scientific, environmental, technological. At the same time, while still in school, they are dealing with serious issues, making choices and confronting dilemmas that previous generations never dreamed of.

Technology, especially telecommunications and computers, has made it possible for young people to know a great deal about their world and what goes on in it, at least on a surface level. They have access to incredible amounts of information, yet much of that information seems irrelevant to their daily lives. When it comes to grappling with the issues that actually touch them, they may have a tough time finding out what they need to know.

The Teenage Perspectives series is designed to give young people access to information on the topics that are closest to their lives or that deeply concern them—topics like families, school, health, sexuality, and drug abuse. Having knowledge about these issues can make it easier to understand and cope with them, and to make appropriate and beneficial choices. The books can be used as tools for researching school assignments, or for finding out about topics of personal concern. Adults who are working with young people, such as teachers, counselors, librarians, and parents, will also find these books useful. Many of the references cited can be used for planning information or discussion sessions with adults as well as young people.

Ruth K. J. Cline
Series Editor

Preface

My motive for writing a book on the career-choice process stems largely from three factors. First of all, I have changed careers a number of times myself, and each time I had to learn from painful experience what seemed to work and not to work in this process. After being approached for advice so often by friends, acquaintances, and others referred to me, I decided to put down some of what I had learned in the hope of making the career search a little easier for others. I especially wanted to reach young people just starting this process and to give them a head start.

In the course of my own career searches, I became aware that, although there were some useful resources on the market, many were sadly out of date. In particular, few resources seemed to be written specifically with young people in mind. I found that many books on career choice were patronizing in tone or were so dull and dry that it was hard to believe they would reach a young audience. Furthermore, since no one book could accomplish everything, it seemed important to include up-to-date references for those motivated to search further.

A second factor prompting this book was my background in assisting young people to test career choices through experiential and cooperative education programs. So many students indicated that they found this career testing valuable and wished they had begun the process earlier, even though these programs happen to be at the university level, that I have made experiential testing of career choices an important theme. No matter what career a person is thinking about, experience with it in volunteer work, internships, or summer jobs can be invaluable, especially before final decisions are made.

The final factor in my decision to write a book for teens on careers is my own years of writing and research in the field of gender issues, particularly on the topic of sex-role stereotyping. I know how restrictive it is when boys and girls are socialized from kindergarten on to think only in terms of the most traditional so-called men's and women's jobs. In the 1990s, we are beginning to move beyond these rigid notions, and it seems appropriate to translate these gains into career choices. Thus, a major theme of this book is to encourage young women and men to look beyond stereotypes and to choose educational tracks and occupations from a much broader field than was ever considered in the past. In an era when so many barriers and myths have tumbled, it seems appropriate to remind young people to be daring and persevering in their career choices, especially today when so much is possible.

Acknowledgments

I have been fortunate to have the valuable assistance of Cheri M. Kaplan, M.Ed., in putting this book together. Drawing on her academic background in counseling psychology and her work in career and counseling centers at college and K–12 grade levels, Kaplan, who is working on her doctorate, contributed to two important chapters: Chapter 2, which covers understanding oneself, as well as psychological and career-testing resources; and Chapter 7, which provides important practical tips to help launch the job search process. In addition, her help in the overall conceptualization and organization served to bring a sharper focus to the entire book.

I also wish to acknowledge the help of Anne Marino, M.S.W., at the University of Southern California, for her intelligent efforts in reviewing the literature and developing early sets of references. Appreciation goes to my daughter Lara Iglitzin, a doctoral student in history at the University of Pennsylvania, and to Janet Looney, a graduate student in the Master of Public Administration (MPA) program at the University of Washington, for their careful and critical reading of the entire manuscript. In addition, I would like to thank my husband, Walter Bodle, a high school classroom teacher, who spent long hours of his precious summer vacation poring over young adult books in the library. His judgment as to what was and what was not suitable to include in the resource lists proved invaluable. And I am grateful to Dorothy Moritz for her help in unraveling the mysteries of word-processing technology.

Finally, I owe a debt of gratitude to the many high school counselors who spent time with me and shared their hopes and frustrations from working in the field of career counseling. These counselors have an enormous task to do, and if this book helps to make their jobs a bit easier, it will more than serve its purpose.

Introduction

Ever since I was a little girl I was fascinated by the kinds of jobs grown-ups did. I was always curious about what my parents did when they were at work. It seemed so mysterious. I was always asking questions about their work, but no one took me very seriously. They always said how cute I was.

Elena, age 14

My older sister, Karen, certainly never received very much "career counseling." Our parents were not very well educated and they didn't encourage her to go to college. So, of course, the first thing she and her boyfriend did when they graduated from high school was to run off and get married. Then she had kids—three by the time she was 20. Career? Her career was diapers and runny noses. I sure want something different for myself, but I'm not sure what.

Laura, age 16

Both my parents are lawyers. There have always been lawyers in our family, and I think everyone has always assumed that I will be one, too. But I'm not so sure. What I really enjoy doing is acting. I have been in every high school production that I could and I loved it. Now I'm ready to graduate and am going on to college. My parents think law school is the next step. But I don't know about that. The head of the drama department says I'm really talented and she has been encouraging me to go to drama school. My

parents will kill me if I say I want to be an actor—
"What kind of a career is that?" I don't know what
I'm going to do.

Eric, age 16

My parents would never admit it, because they think
they are encouraging me to follow my own interests
no matter what, but I know they really want me to go
into a career where the money is good. Whenever I
mention that I might like to go into some humanitar-
ian thing and work with abused kids or the homeless,
my parents look uncomfortable. I know they are
thinking, "Why don't you go for a job that will earn
enough to pay for all that expensive college tuition
we'll be footing the bill for?"

Victor, age 15

Elena, Laura, Eric, and Victor shared their thoughts about
careers and aspirations in response to a visitor's questions. As
part of my preparation for this book, I spent a year talking to
students, guidance counselors, and parents to get a sense of the
view of young people in the 1990s about life after high school.

The answers I got were not very encouraging. Most of the
juniors and seniors with whom I talked have little or no idea of
what they want to "be" when they grow up. When asked
directly, many are reluctant to answer and they lower their
eyes. Embarrassed, their teachers urge them to answer, to say
something, to give the visitor researching her book some
answer—any answer. And so the answers start to come. Disc
jockey . . . engineer . . . neurosurgeon . . . businessman . . . computer specialist. But somehow these seem to be spur-of-the-
moment answers, designed to please the teacher and not really
thought out.

"And what do you want to get out of your career?" I ask.
Almost invariably, the first answer is, "Money!" Some go on to
name free time or power, but most have not really thought
about this question. It seems these high school students are not

thinking much about careers at all. This seems to hold true whether the students are making straight A's and are college bound or whether they are barely hanging in, waiting for high school to be over so they can get a job—any job that will allow them to leave home and be on their own.

This impression was borne out by my interviews with high school guidance counselors. A guidance counselor at an inner-city school in a large city told me she spends less than 5 percent of her time on career counseling. Most of her time is spent trying to help young people stay in school and, in a few cases, to set their sights on more education, at least at a community college or in a vocational training program. The problem, she explained, is a lack of adult role models in challenging and interesting jobs. As a result, students' aspirations are traditional and sex-stereotyped. Boys want to go into sports, and girls talk about being beauticians or nurses.

In contrast, at a school in the affluent hills of a Northwestern suburb, more than 90 percent of the students will go on to college. Yet, the counselor tells me, there is practically no interest in career or vocational counseling here either. Although hers is the only school I visit that has a well-stocked career resource center, this counselor tells me it is seldom used by any of the students. They are thinking about college; if their parents are thinking about their children's careers at all, it is only to hope that someday their kids will earn enough to help pay for those expensive college educations! These students are so focused on getting into college that neither they nor their parents have time or energy left to think about what lies beyond. And, like their counterparts across town, they are intent on one goal: to make money!

Still another counselor tells me that students have a lot of anxiety, both about college and about computers. Here, too, the students hardly ever use the school's career resource materials. They seem to have little idea what their options really are beyond the usual general fields, with the exception of computers. Computers are "in," the counselor says, and this makes those who are fearful about their computing and math abilities, or those who might simply be drawn to other fields such as the arts or human services, prone to even more anxiety. "If I can't do computers, what good will I be?" seems to be the new refrain.

It was with all these thoughts on my mind that I sat down to write a book to help young people focus on their career and occupational choices in the years ahead. The time I spent talking with teenagers led me to the book's central theme: Choosing a career needs to be a careful and thoughtful process. You do not simply look in the classified ads to see what jobs are available on any given day. And you do not pick a career because you admire a glamorous television newscaster or a successful rock music star. Instead, you try to figure out a way to explore the vast number of options open to you and the many directions you might go.

If you are lucky, you will not be entirely on your own in this process. As you read this book, you are encouraged to talk about your ideas with your friends, parents, teachers, librarians, counselors, and especially people you know who are doing work that seems interesting to you. As you continue on this exploratory path, things that seem overwhelming at first will steadily become clearer.

The chapters in this book are designed to help you focus on your career in two ways: by asking you to look at yourself and to look at the world around you. Chapter 1 begins the process by describing some of the reasons people work, from needing money to get the basics of life, such as food and shelter, to wanting to satisfy other, less tangible but still important, needs such as self-esteem. The end of high school is probably the first big turning point in your life, and even though it is scary to realize it, you are about to make some major decisions that will affect you for years to come.

In Chapter 2 you will be asked to do perhaps the hardest thing of all: to take a long, hard look at who you are. All career and educational planning needs to begin with the process of learning and knowing your interests, skills, values, and the family influences that have molded you. If you don't know yourself, you cannot possibly make the choices that will be best for you.

Chapter 3 asks you to shift the focus from yourself to the world around you. In particular you will look at the rapid changes occurring in the workplace, the ways in which computers are revolutionizing the workplace, and what this means to you. We'll also look at the trends affecting the work force:

Who are the workers of today? Of tomorrow? And where do you fit into all of this?

Chapter 4 explores the job market, with an overview of the many different kinds of jobs and occupations that people have. This chapter covers some steps you can take to begin the research necessary to find out what careers and opportunities sound both interesting and possible for you.

Once you have made some tentative choices about your career direction, you are ready to look at the many career-preparation options. These are discussed in Chapters 5 and 6. Chapter 5 covers the traditional routes of college, university, and vocational-training education. Chapter 6 covers avenues that place emphasis less on the classroom and more on on-the-job training and work experience.

Chapter 7 gives some practical tips for getting started in the job search. Chapter 8 again examines the workplace, this time from the important perspective of moving toward a goal of equal opportunity. We are especially interested in how women and minorities can expect to fare in the job market of the 1990s and the years beyond.

Finally, Chapter 9 pulls all the threads together and asks you to think long and hard about how you can most successfully blend your personal and family needs with the world of work.

As you prepare to leave high school and to move on in the world, you are indeed at a major turning point in your life. If this book helps you think about all the issues involved in making career choices, it will have met its goal. I have tried to include a great many references for you to use, fiction and nonfiction, print and film. Sometimes you will want to consult a directory of jobs or college programs, and these references are included. Other times, you will learn more by reading an auto-biography or watching a movie about someone you admire in a field in which you are interested. The variety of sources, I believe, will prove useful in your explorations. And do take the time to read the brief annotations for each of the references; they will give you an immediate sense of just how helpful or interesting the resource will be to you.

Starting the process of career choice and planning is like the beginning of any journey. You need to decide where you want to go, for how long, how much time and preparation are required, and what kind of equipment you will need. You are understandably anxious to start right in, but, as with any journey, taking the time for thought and preparation pays off in the long run and prevents costly mistakes later. You are about to embark on one of the most important journeys you have ever made: an exploration of the world of work and the many ways in which you might fit into this world.

Good luck and bon voyage!

CHAPTER 1

You and the World of Work: Life beyond High School

Endings and Beginnings

The final exam . . . the senior prom . . . cleaning out your locker
. . . writing that special message in the yearbook. Whether you
are in ninth grade and looking forward to four years in high
school, or in the last months of your senior year with graduation almost upon you, you know that completion of high
school marks an ending. It is probably the most significant
milestone in your life up to now.

If you have gotten this far, you have undoubtedly put a
great deal of work into your studies. Perhaps you have com-
bined academics with sports or other extracurricular activities.
Maybe you have worked part-time or during the summer while
going to school to earn your own money. However you have
done it, you have been focused pretty much on one thing:
getting through school.

So, while it may seem like asking a lot of you to think
about what comes next, it is important that you realize that
there is life after high school! In fact, for years and years your
life will involve some combination of working, playing, studying, traveling, and engaging in family activities. Completion of
high school is an ending, yes, but it is also a beginning. And
this book will help you focus on beginning the next stage of
your life: your 40–50 years as a working person.

With all its troubles and difficulties, high school has been
familiar to you. You have known what was expected of you and
what the next day, week, or month was likely to bring. While
you have had decisions to make, they have been made within

the known context of high school. Turning to adults such as teachers and guidance counselors for advice, you have made choices between this class and that one, this course of study or another. But now you are faced with major choices, indeed. These choices are sure to affect much of your adult life, as well as the people with whom you will be sharing your life.

As an adult, you will make all kinds of choices among options. Many of these relate to the personal aspects of your life. You will decide such important things as whether to get married or stay single, have children, live in the city or the country, near or far from parents and grandparents. You will consider all kinds of life-style options, and will undoubtedly change your mind and your choices often—far more often than you might expect.

The focus in this book is on one major area in which you will make choices: careers and occupations. Notice that we use the plural here. Right from the beginning we want you to realize that, probably in contrast to your parents and grandparents, throughout your many productive working years you may well have several different careers. This is another reason to get a head start on how and why choices are made.

Who Works and Why: The Basic Reasons

Congratulations! You have just won the lottery, and won big. Your winnings entitle you to so much money each year, even after taxes, that you do not "need to work" for the rest of your life. That sounds pretty good to just about anyone.

But even if you won the lottery, you would still have choices to make. Choices about how to spend your time, with whom, and doing what. A lot of the decisions you would make would reflect who you are and the values and beliefs you hold dear.

You might well choose to work, despite the fact that you did not need to. All people have basic needs or drives, and many of these are best fulfilled by doing some type of productive work. The fact that you have won the lottery would simply mean that you would not be forced by financial factors to work. Most people work, first of all, because they have to—they must be able to support themselves and maybe some family members. They have to earn enough to buy food, shelter, and the other necessities of life. Not surprisingly, if given the choice, a great many people would choose an occupation that seems to promise material security over one that might be more satisfying, but less secure and predictable.

Why We Work: Beyond the Basics

Working to earn a living is basic, but it is only the first level of our needs. Once these basic needs for food on the table and a roof over one's head are met, other needs can be considered. Working serves to meet many of them.

Work is a major source of identity for most adults. It is not uncommon that the first question asked when you meet someone new is, "And what do you do?"

Work fills another important human need: personal dignity. The most common refrain among chronically out-of-work people, even as they line up for their unemployment benefits and food stamps (which help them meet their basic wants), is that they want to work. Very few people like to be on welfare and dependent on others, whether it be the state, their parents, or their children. Status in the community is related in part to the type of work people do and how well they are viewed as doing it. Most people like to feel that they are productive members of society.

If your work not only puts bread on your table but is also satisfying, then you are fortunate indeed. Your job helps to fulfill another important human need: self-esteem. High morale and job satisfaction may mean as much as, or more than, the actual dollars in a paycheck.

One source of this sense of job satisfaction and self-esteem is the feeling that you are fully utilizing your skills and abilities. You get pleasure and a sense of accomplishment in doing a job you like when you know you have given your best effort and done the work as well as you could. When your occupation allows you to receive appreciation and recognition from your bosses and co-workers, it plays a vital role in meeting your need for self-esteem.

Most of us also want our jobs to meet other needs. The intensity of these needs varies among individuals, but nonetheless there are feelings we share. Many people want some control over their work lives or have a strong need for flexible schedules. They want time for "R&R," because this rest and relaxation help them cope with work life. Others have a strong need for prestige, status, and influence, and see these as intangible benefits some jobs give. Still others look for more tangible benefits such as travel, bonuses, expense accounts, or the corner office with a view.

Career Decisions *Are* Important

Another factor contributing to your satisfaction with the work you do is your feeling that it is useful to society. Virtually every type of job and occupation benefits society in some way. The doctor, the auto mechanic, the schoolteacher, and the construction worker all help make other people's lives easier or more efficient. Depending on your skills and inclinations, you may be drawn to occupations in which you work with people; if you are mechanically or scientifically inclined, you might be attracted by the challenge of building bridges or spacecraft. All of these kinds of occupations and skills are important to others.

Society needs some people who are willing to become involved in less clear-cut and more difficult areas, where the challenges are high. These people dedicate themselves to helping make the world a better place to live. A career that fuels social change is satisfying for some people. Increasingly, as we get further into the 1990s, we find more young people seeking careers in which they can be of service to others. As you read the newspapers and go about your daily life, you cannot escape awareness of the major societal problems of poverty, homelessness, drug abuse, gangs, overcrowded cities, and environmental pollution. The satisfaction of helping to make life better for a single mother and her children, or being part of a team working to improve the quality of the air in your city, may be its own reward. Of course, the ideal job is one that meets your own personal needs and also helps society.

Whatever needs motivate you and affect your choice of career or occupation, those decisions will influence every aspect of your life thereafter. Our jobs help determine the friends we have, where we live, and our leisure-time activities. So the decisions about work and careers are really major ones, perhaps far more important than you had realized. Getting a part-time job in the neighborhood supermarket for extra cash is one thing. Choosing an occupation in which you will spend many hours a day for many years is quite another. And successfully turning a "job" into a "career" with steadily increasing responsibilities and opportunities for advancement, growth, and fulfillment is yet another important goal.

When you finally leave the classroom, whether it be after high school or college or some other training, and enter an occupation full-time, you will undoubtedly think of yourself for the first time as an adult. Others will probably see you that way as well. This is not surprising, since having a job usually means that you are independent and in control of where and how you live your life. If you also experience a sense of enjoyment and fulfillment in your job, you tend to work harder, feel more personally involved, and take more adult responsibility. Your career choices affect the way others see you and feel about you, but most importantly, they affect how you feel about yourself.

High School: Is That Diploma Really Necessary?

An important theme throughout this book is the need to obtain as much education and training as possible to equip you for your career choices in a complex world. All this talk about education and schooling may not make you happy, especially if you are getting tired of high school and wondering when you are going to get out and enter an occupation in the "real" world. Perhaps you are wondering why you should even bother to finish high school, much less plan to get more education and training. Let's respond to some of these thoughts in a way that seems most appropriate for school: a true-or-false test.

1. "High school has little to do with the real world. It is just a way of keeping me out of trouble until I am old enough to earn a living." FALSE!

2. "There are lots of jobs out there, many with good salaries. A high school diploma is just a piece of paper; the sooner I get out and start working, the faster I can move up the job ladder." FALSE!
3. "I'll never get a good job anyway, unless I go to college, and there is no way I want to do that, or could afford to go." FALSE!

As you can see, each of these ideas is "false." One of the purposes of this book is to dispel the myth that what you study in high school has little to do with your future in a job or career. In fact, just the reverse is true. The skills you learn in high school—reading, writing, computing, analyzing, and logical thinking—are basic to your survival and success in every job, from the simplest to the most complicated.

In high school you learn the discipline of good study and work habits. You learn that it takes hard work to complete your objective of passing that math or English class. And you learn the need for perseverance in working out regularly to meet your goals in gymnastics or football. These kinds of goal-setting and work habits are valued highly in the work world. When you show an employer your high school diploma, you are showing evidence that you have succeeded in completing an important milestone.

High school is also useful as a testing time to get a sense of the things you like and do well, and the areas you find boring or difficult. These are important clues for career testing. The broader the range of courses you take in high school, the better prepared you will be for whatever directions your career may take later in life. Job opportunities may open up in new and unpredictable ways, and your own interests and goals may change as well. If you have a good math and science background, for example, you will be in a better position to succeed in many of the high-technology fields such as computer science and engineering. You will also need a good math background for college-entrance exams.

There are probably times when you get really discouraged and feel like dropping out of school. Schoolwork may seem overwhelming or you may be under family or financial pressures to get a job. The best advice anyone can give you—and everyone *will* give you—is: *Stay in school!* Statistics show that most teenagers who leave school without a diploma end up in dead-end, low-paying jobs. And many find themselves without jobs at all. As we know, automation is eliminating many of the unskilled jobs that used to be filled by people with limited education. Graduation from high school will help keep your options as wide as possible.

You may be surprised to learn that the consequences of dropping out are rather dramatic, especially when viewed over time. Here are some findings published by the U.S. Department of Education:

> Dropouts have more difficulty finding and holding jobs.
>
> Those who do not finish high school earn less money annually than high school graduates.
>
> The estimated lifetime earnings of high school graduates who do not attend college are approximately $200,000 higher than the earnings of those who do not complete high school.

If you are unhappy in school, try to figure out what your problems are and see if you can get help. Leaving school is rarely the way to solve your problems, whether they are bad grades, the need to earn money, or family pressures. The chances are that if you ask, someone—a teacher, a guidance counselor, a social worker, or a parent—will try to help you find ways to deal with your concerns. Keep in mind that a lot of doors will be closed to you if you do not graduate from high school.

Crossroads: Which Way To Go?

Graduation from high school is both an ending and a beginning; that is why it is such an important milestone in every young person's life. Of course, the exciting thing about any milestone is that you are poised to take the next step. But the next step is not only exciting, it is scary. As you approach high school graduation, like the traveler at the intersection of two major highways, you are at a crossroads. Which path do you take? Facing this decision can be even more daunting now that you realize that your choice of occupation is far more important than simply choosing a way to bring in a paycheck. Clearly, career decisions determine all sorts of things about how you will live your life.

Which career path should you take? What are you good at? What do you like to do? What kinds of jobs will be available when you are ready to enter the job market? What training or education will you need? There are thousands of jobs out there. How can you begin to make sense of the options that will be open to you? To make matters worse, new jobs seem to pop up each day. As technology rapidly revolutionizes the workplace, we can hardly keep up with new job fields such as robotics, biogenetics, or telecommunications. How can you possibly figure out what people who work in those areas do, much less decide if you would like to do it, whatever "it" is?

So you are at a crossroads, trying to make up your mind whether to go to college, what kind of courses to take, whether to enroll in a technical-training program, or whether to go directly into the job market. As any good driver knows, when you're at an intersection the best way to go is to look in all directions, watch the signals, and then move forward cautiously. Your career path can be relatively smooth or it can be full of potholes, depending on how good your planning is and the route you choose. Of course, there are potholes lying in wait in everyone's path; the better planner you are the more chances you have to avoid the bumps in the road. The trick is to make the choices that are best for you and to avoid stumbling in the potholes and getting stuck at dead ends along the way.

This trip begins with a journey of self-discovery and then moves to the discovery of the outside world. Think of yourself as an explorer charting unknown territories, for they are unknown to you. You will first need to explore who you are: what you like to do, what your strengths and talents are, and what is important to you. You will be gathering information about the world of work at the same time.

You will find it useful to keep a loose-leaf notebook for your career planning. In the back include a folder to hold articles from magazines and newspapers about people doing interesting work. Try to figure out why you cut out the article, that is, why this or that occupation seems appealing. In the notebook write down observations, quotations, book titles, and the various exercises you will complete during the career planning process.

The Time Is Now: The Choices Are Yours

Whoever you are, wherever you live, and whatever your dreams and aspirations, you are fortunate to have the opportunity to choose from the many fascinating careers and occupations available today. In the 1990s, we are benefitting from a more open society that is coming to recognize that gender, age, race, or physical disability need not automatically close off any career. You have a much broader field from which to choose than your parents or grandparents had.

You can expect to work for more than 40 years. You owe it to yourself to ensure that those years are as fulfilling and satisfying as possible. Your workday need not be routine and dull. It can be a source of continual learning and even pleasure from the first day you set foot in a new job. Now is the time to begin to think about the areas that will best match your abilities and interests. As a teenager, you have the opportunity to explore every aspect of work and to make sound decisions about the future.

With careful thought, planning, and research, you should be able to choose a career that is right for you at any particular time. Keep in mind, moreover, that you may have more than one career during your life. As you grow, there will be inevitable changes in your interests and needs, and these will affect what you are looking for in an occupation at those different points in your life. Thus, it is important that you view the process of gathering information about yourself and the many possible career paths as something that will continue throughout your working life.

This book will help you set goals and aim for them. It will assist you in matching your skills and aptitudes with an appropriate occupation. And it will give you practical suggestions

for preparing for a variety of work experiences, from apprenticeships and entry-level jobs to higher-level positions down
the road. The choices are yours.

REFERENCES

Fowler, Elizabeth M. *The New York Times Career Planner*. New
York: Times Books, 1987.

Lewis, Adele, William Lewis, and Steven Radlauer. *How To
Choose, Change, Advance Your Career*. New York: Barron's
Educational Series, 1983.

Maccoby, Michael. *Why Work: Leading the New Generation*. New
York: Simon and Schuster, 1988.

Michelozzi, Betty. *Coming Alive from Nine to Five*. 3d ed.
Mountain View, CA: Mayfield Press, 1988.

Pallas, Aaron M., "School Dropouts in the United States," *The
Condition of Education*. 1986 ed., 158–174.

Pilder, Richard J., and William F. Pilder. *How To Find Your Life's
Work*. Englewood Cliffs, NJ: Prentice-Hall, 1981.

U.S. Department of Education, National Center for Education
Statistics. *Digest of Education Statistics 1985–86*. Washington, DC:
U.S. Government Printing Office, 1986.

Resources

for Finding Out about You and the World of Work

Fiction

Bach, Richard. **One.** New York: Dell, 1988. 378p.

The author of *Jonathan Livingston Seagull* has written an imaginative and thought-provoking book about how the choices we make affect our lives. The main character and his wife embark on a fictional journey in a seaplane that touches down in various universes, and they meet alternate versions of themselves. A hopeful and inspirational book that will appeal to young adults facing life choices.

Franklin, Miles. **My Brilliant Career.** New York: St. Martin's, 1980. 232p.

The heroine of this novel, set in rural Australia, lived at the turn of the century, but her story is as current as the 1990s. The novel contrasts the struggle for survival in the harsh climate with a young woman's yearning for art, music, and literature. The story of how she persists despite overwhelming odds and begins to create her own career as a writer is truly inspirational.

LeGuin, Ursula K. **Very Far Away from Anywhere Else.** New York: MacMillan, 1976. 89p.

Owen desperately wants to become a great scientist, against his parents' wishes, and he despairs of being understood. He meets Natalie, a true nonconformist who wants to become an actress and refuses to compromise her career plans. A strong and realistically drawn story about teenagers whose career dreams conflict with their parents' ideas.

Pfeffer, Susan B. **Getting Even.** Berkeley: Pacer, 1986. 188p.

Annie has an exciting summer and then must return to the mundane routine of school. She finds a job as an assistant in a public relations office and acquires a new boyfriend. Through her mistakes, she learns to be sensitive to the needs of other people. Interesting reading for someone wrestling with job and school concerns.

Wersba, Barbara. **The Farewell Kid.** New York: Harper & Row, 1990. 155p.

Eighteen-year-old Heidi sets out on her own, moves into her own apartment, and opens a dog-rescue business. As Heidi struggles to maintain her business, and more importantly her independence, she meets Harvey, who is also attempting to find himself. A good story illustrating the self-discovery, joys, and perils of striking out on your own.

Nonfiction

BOOKS

Johnston, Neil. **All in a Day's Work: Twelve Americans Talk about Their Jobs.** New York: Joy Street Books, 1989. 89p.

From detective to TV journalist, judge to assembly-line worker, individuals speak passionately and honestly about their work and what it means to them in the context of their lives. The book offers a fascinating glimpse into how Americans find meaning and value in what they do at work.

Kennedy, Joyce Lain. **Career Book.** Lincolnwood, IL: National Textbook, 1988. 424p.

A comprehensive career guide designed for young adults. This book is intended for those preparing for college as well as those seeking careers immediately. Career planning is a family affair, and much here will be helpful to parents and counselors working with teens.

Males, Carolyn, and Roberta Feigen. **Life after High School.** New York: Julian Messner, 1986. 176p.

A practical planning guide, especially for those who have no idea which fields they want to consider. This book is designed to take some of the scariness out of making career choices by helping you discover what you are good at, and showing you how to explore different occupations.

Michelozzi, Betty. **Coming Alive from Nine to Five: The Career Search Handbook.** 3d ed. Mountain View, CA: Mayfield Press, 1988. 300p.

A useful book to help you determine your skills, strengths, and weaknesses. Includes self-testing and self-scoring activities.

Moyers, Bill. **A World of Ideas: Conversations with Thoughtful Men and Women.** 1st ed. New York: Doubleday, 1989. 513p.

One-on-one interviews with 42 men and women from various walks of life, including poets, historians, novelists, doctors, scientists, educators, and others. The interviews cover a range of topics and contain much reflection and discussion on careers. This book is ideal for browsing and an excellent way to begin thinking about interesting people and occupations.

Terkel, Studs. **Working.** New York: Pantheon, 1974. 768p.

Conversations with ordinary people about "what they do all day and how they feel about what they do." The result is an extraordinary collection of unique voices, past and present, as people from many walks of life speak candidly about working and living. Still relevant years after it was written, this book provides a good way to begin thinking about what kinds of jobs would and would not appeal to you.

Wirths, Claudine G., and Mary Bowman-Kruhm. **I Hate School: How To Hang In and When To Drop Out.** New York: Harper & Row/Trophy, 1986. 115p.

A book for those who may be fed up with school and thinking of dropping out. This is a good book to consult before making any final decision to leave school. It contains practical advice, suggestions on how to take charge of your life, and useful information on some alternatives to high school. It also includes practical tips to help you hang in and pass your courses.

Nonprint Materials

Dropout Prevention: Being Your Personal Best
Type: VHS video
Length: 20 min.
Cost: Rental $50; purchase $395
Source: AIMS Media
            6901 Woodley Avenue
            Van Nuys, CA 91406-4878
            (800) 367-2467

As a teenager, Kelly was one of the 25 percent nationwide who dropped out of school. Finding it difficult to make it in the world, she returned to school for her diploma. Now she works to keep young people from making the same mistake she did. Candid discussions and dramatic flashbacks help the viewer set goals and gain self-esteem. A good film for anyone going through doubts and uncertainties about themselves and their abilities.

Is There Life after High School? Planning Your Future
Type: VHS video
Length: 45 min. (3 parts)
Cost: Purchase $175
Source: Guidance Associates
            Communications Park
            Box 3000
            Mt. Kisco, NY 10549-9989
            (800) 431-1242
Date: 1990

A comprehensive overview of options available after high school graduation. This video covers the importance of marketable skills and the various ways to prepare for a career, including college and other types of apprenticeship and training programs.

My Brilliant Career
Type: VHS video
Length: 101 min.
Cost: Standard rental charge
Source: Regular video outlets
Date: 1979

The heroine of this feature film, set in rural Australia, lived at the turn of the century, but her story is as current as the 1990s. The film contrasts the struggle for survival in this harsh climate with a young woman's yearning for art, music, and literature. The story of how she persists despite overwhelming odds and begins to create her own career as a writer is truly inspirational. Based on the novel by Miles Franklin.

The Power of Choice
Type: VHS video
Length: 60 min.
Cost: Not available
Source: Live Wire Video Publishers
           3315 Sacramento Street
           San Francisco, CA 94118
Date: 1989

Designed to help teenagers make choices based upon their best vision of themselves rather than out of fear, guilt, or spite. Michael Pritchard, a teen counselor and stand-up comic, interacts with high school students in various group settings on specific problems and dilemmas. Issues such as peer pressure, self-esteem, and relationships with parents are relevant to the career-exploration process.

Soapbox with Tom Cottle: High School Dropouts
Type: VHS video
Length: 30 min.
Cost: Purchase $59.95

Source: PBS Video
            1320 Braddock Place
            Alexandria, VA 22314-1698
            (800) 424-7963
Date: 1985

More than 25 percent of all teens drop out of high school. This video asks teens why they feel the need to quit and raises the question of whether the lure of a job can compensate for the loss of a diploma. Discusses some of the dilemmas that face those who don't finish high school.

Why Work?
Type: VHS video
Length: 26 min.
Cost: Rental $50; purchase $200
Source: Journal Films, Inc.
            930 Pitner Avenue
            Evanston, IL 60602
            (800) 323-5448
Date: 1983

Traces the nature of work in the last 100 years, and deals particularly with the concept of the Protestant work ethic.

CHAPTER 2

Understanding Careers: Looking within You

With Cheri M. Kaplan

Your Family, Yourself

Who are you? Part of the answer can be found by looking at your family. Early childhood experiences and family patterns influence each of us. As we begin to create an identity for ourselves we look to our parents, grandparents, brothers, sisters, and other relatives as role models for our decisions. Their opinions make an impression. Their attitudes help to shape our own. The careers they have chosen have an impact on the choices we will make.

Families may encourage the development of specific interests and abilities very early in a child's life, particularly when a career involves unique skills and long years of training. For example, famous musicians often come from homes where not only their parents but even their grandparents have been musicians. The children get musical instruction from a very early age and grow up in an environment where music seems as natural as breathing. Quite often, those raised in such a household grow into professionals without being able to identify a point at which they actually made that decision.

When you are young it is common to want to be "just like" your mom or dad when you grow up, and some people do follow closely in the footsteps of one of their parents. Milt McColl of the Los Angeles Raiders did so in an unusual way. In his eighth-grade yearbook he wrote that he hoped to be a professional athlete. This was not a surprise; Milt's father played pro football. What was more surprising was that Milt not only followed his father's athletic path, winning a football scholarship to Stanford University and starring on Stanford's football team, as his dad had done, but he also followed a parallel career in medicine. Today, he is pursuing his medical studies with the goal of becoming an orthopedic surgeon, just like his father.

You may well be influenced by your parents even if you do not follow precisely in their career paths. In an article in *The New Yorker*, marine biologist Sylvia Earle described how she was influenced by her parents, neither of whom were scientists. Earle explained how their values and attitudes guided her own choices. She credits her interest in wild things to her mother, whom she describes as having a natural rapport with the world around her.

"Unlike a lot of parents, she would never say, 'Yuk! Don't touch that slimy thing!' Instead, she'd bring a snake into the house and say, 'Isn't this an elegant creature? Touch it gently, because it is very sensitive.' And it wasn't zoology, at least not in any formal way. It was just an empathy for life." Sylvia Earle credits her interest in marine biology to these formative years and to her parents' encouragement and values.

It is more common, however, for struggle and indecision to be part of the career decision-making process. Often parents' opinions and ideas can be a source of stress and conflict. Ultimately, it is your own responsibility to choose the paths you take. Your family may be influential in your decision making, but only you can make the decisions.

As you think about the careers you would like to explore, be aware of how the opinions of your family affect you. This family influence may be helpful; however, in some cases it may be limiting. Understanding the ways in which your family has shaped your identity is crucial for living a healthy existence. Part of growing up is the process of trying to separate your own needs, values, and interests from those your parents would like you to have. In order to make healthy choices for yourself throughout your life you must be aware of your own identity and how you have been influenced. As you develop and explore various careers, focus on who you are and what is important to you.

Getting To Know Yourself: A Personal Inventory

Getting to know yourself may seem easy. After all, if you don't know yourself, who does? Although this may appear to be the case, it is common to find that people never really take the time to look at themselves. In order to grow, you must first understand who you are. It may not be easy, but it is important. As you read this chapter, you may want to jot down notes in your career notebook.

A good place to start getting to know yourself is to look back over your life. Think about your education, your hobbies, and any previous work experience you have had. What aspects of these jobs did you like and which did you dislike? It may be helpful to list the academic courses you have taken, activities you have been part of, and jobs you have held, and to write down your reactions to these experiences. As you review your life you will begin to see patterns. Becoming aware of these patterns is the first step toward understanding yourself. The best way to begin this process is to identify your interests, values, and skills.

Interests are those things you like to do. You may like to write, read, help others, raise money, debate, create things, or fix things. List all the things in which you are interested. Don't hold anything back. Too many people do not consider their interests when they make career decisions. A hobby you enjoy today may be the beginning of an exciting career. Imagine that for the rest of your life you could do anything you wanted (don't worry about money); what would you do?

Values are the beliefs about life that are important to you. Different people have different values. One person may believe status is the most important thing, another may feel a high income is crucial, and still another may strive to achieve social change. Values may be the deciding factor in your career choice. As you continue to mature and grow throughout your life, your values may change. What values are important to you now? Here are some for you to begin thinking about.

Helping society

Helping others

Competition

Power and authority

Monetary status

Intellectual status

Security

Change and variety

Stability

Aesthetics

Independence

Artistic creativity

Recognition

Adventure

Influencing others

Skills are the last area to include in your personal inventory. Each person has unique skills and abilities; identifying your strengths provides you the chance to develop them through training, education, and, eventually, employment. Have you been complimented on particular skills or abilities? You may wish to make a list of your skills. Generally, employers look for some combination of the following skills. Can you identify with any of these?

Communication

Leadership

Problem-solving

Confidence

Creativity

Goal achievement

Interpersonal skills

Responsibility

Flexibility

Time management

Conflict resolution

Stress management

Organization

Analytical skills

Choosing a career is not a once-in-a-lifetime decision; as you develop and change, your career will change too. It is important to continue to assess your interests, skills, and values throughout your lifespan.

Psychologists have divided interests, values, and skills into six categories: realistic, investigative, artistic, social, enterprising, and conventional. Think about which categories you fit into; you may well fit into more than one, and you do not have to meet all the characteristics to fit into a category.

These categories should be used loosely. They are meant to help you think of possibilities, not to delete options. Begin to think about how your interests, values, and skills relate to possible careers. Use your imagination. We've given you some examples to get you started.

REALISTIC

Interests

The realistic category includes individuals who enjoy building and rebuilding things; using equipment; repairing old things; refinishing furniture; reading books and magazines about outdoor sports, cars, airplanes, and boats; or participating in physically dangerous activities such as skydiving, auto racing, or mountain climbing.

Self-Concept and Values

These people are reliable, emotionally stable, practical, thrifty, persistent, shy, and modest. They may be adventurous and inclined to take physical risks. They are likely to have traditional values.

Skills

Realistic people have mechanical skills, manual dexterity, good psychomotor skills, and mathematical aptitude.

Careers

Careers in this category include: carpenter, rancher, engineer, forester, pilot, veterinarian, welder, appliance repairer, fire fighter, warehouse worker, exterminator, occupational therapist, architect, construction worker, law-enforcement officer, farmer, military personnel, truck driver, auto mechanic, electronics technician, and craftsperson.

INVESTIGATIVE

Interests

Individuals in the investigative group enjoy pursuing things that raise curiosity, such as working with computers, reading, astronomy, using a chemistry set, playing chess, solving puzzles, and bird watching.

Self-Concept and Values

Investigative people are independent, self-motivated, reserved, analytical, curious, task-oriented, original, and creative. They are confident of their scholarly and intellectual abilities, and they generally have unconventional values.

Skills

Those in this category have good scientific and mathematical ability; analytical, writing, and interpretation skills; and problem-solving, observational, and evaluation skills.

Careers

Some choices are: biologist, chemist, geographer, mathematician, economist, anthropologist, psychologist, physician, dentist, engineer, pharmacist, computer operator, computer programmer, chiropractor, systems analyst, math or science teacher, and lawyer.

ARTISTIC

Interests

Artistic individuals enjoy drawing, painting, sketching, sculpting, pottery, and photography. They like to attend dance and musical concerts or go to theaters, museums, and galleries. They may like reading, writing poetry or short stories, collecting art work, and dancing.

Self-Concept and Values

Artistic types are independent, impulsive, expressive, impractical, intuitive, nonconforming, sensitive, and emotional. They are drawn to beauty, artistic creativity, and aesthetic qualities.

Skills

Skills include creativity, imagination, and artistic aptitude. This type is usually adept at one or more of the following: playing an instrument, singing, acting, dancing, painting, sculpting, designing clothes, writing poetry, or composing music.

Careers

Career choices for the artistic category would be: artist, musician, actor, author, photographer, music teacher, English teacher, philosopher, public relations specialist, or fashion model. Other possibilities are: gallery owner, illustrator, art administrator, museum administrator, fashion illustrator, production designer for film and television, video graphics designer, cartoonist, publications designer, industrial designer, department store art director, mural painter, fashion display specialist, city planner, or interior decorator. Persons in this category might also choose to be: ballet dancer, stage and set designer, writer, art teacher, orchestra conductor, advertising executive, librarian, reporter, costume designer, landscape gardener, architect, or anthropologist.

SOCIAL

Interests

Those in the social category are interested in doing volunteer and community service work, organizing group social events, entertaining others, helping others with problems, and caring for children and elders.

Self-Concept and Values

This group values being humanistic, idealistic, ethical, responsible, cooperative, kind, generous, insightful, and understanding. These individuals are concerned for the welfare of others and value helping society, being altruistic, and developing personal relationships.

Skills

Skills found in this category are social, interpersonal, and communication skills. This group has teaching aptitude and the ability to explain, guide, inform, organize, and listen effectively.

Careers

Careers for the social category include: teacher, nurse, juvenile parole officer, child care center manager, community education coordinator, mental-health worker, guidance counselor, school administrator, rehabilitation counselor, social worker, student personnel worker, training director, therapist, speech pathologist, recreation director, and physical-education instructor.

ENTERPRISING

Interests

The enterprising category contains those who enjoy belonging to clubs and organizations, attending sporting events, entertaining, vacationing, and partying. These people are politically active and enjoy running their own businesses and debating.

Self-Concept and Values

This type is status-conscious, ambitious, competitive, sociable, talkative, argumentative, domineering, and aggressive. They may be adventurous, risk-taking, optimistic, energetic, and popular. They are attracted to money, power, and material possessions.

Skills

Enterprising individuals use their verbal skills for public speaking, persuading, selling, and presentations. They also have social, interpersonal, and leadership skills. They are energetic, enthusiastic, good debaters, and competent at organizing and managing projects.

Careers

Good career choices for this category are: beautician, auctioneer, elected public official, life-insurance agent, personnel director, restaurant manager, salesperson, buyer, corporate executive, investments manager, marketing executive, sales manager, flight attendant, stockbroker, contractor, personnel recruiter, insurance underwriter, receptionist, and lawyer.

CONVENTIONAL

Interests

Among interests of the conventional type are collecting stamps or coins; building models, electric trains, and dollhouses; home-improvement projects; and playing games.

Self-Concept and Values

This type is practical, conscientious, conservative, self-controlled, orderly, systematic, precise, accurate, careful, and inflexible. Their values include stability, money, and material possessions.

Skills

Conventional people often have manual dexterity and mathematical aptitude. They are organized, efficient, and perfectionistic.

Careers

Good career choices for this type are: accountant, bookkeeper, proofreader, secretary, statistician, key-punch operator, cashier, banker, credit manager, Internal Revenue Service agent, court reporter, dental assistant, financial expert, estimator, data processor, office manager, executive housekeeper, business-education teacher, library assistant, telephone operator, time-keeper, and public administrator.

Feeling Stuck? Career Testing May Help

If you find that you are unable to think clearly about your interests, skills, and values you can seek out objective tests to help you clarify your thoughts. Psychologists have created standardized assessments that can assist you in self-exploration. Tests help you tap into your aptitude, achievement, and vocational interests.

Aptitude tests generally measure your potential. Some of the more popular aptitude tests are the Scholastic Aptitude Test (SAT), the American College Test, and the Differential Aptitude Test. Achievement tests measure what you have learned. Two well-known achievement tests are the College Board Achievement Test and the Comprehensive Test of Basic Skills.

Vocational-interest tests measure your interests and compare them with individuals who are currently in various occupations. Some popular tests are the Strong-Campbell Interest Inventory, the California Occupational Preference Survey (COPS), the Myers Briggs Type Indicator and Self-Directed Search, and the System of Interactive Guidance and Information Plus (SIGI+).

These assessments are used as starting points. They are helpful as an objective confirmation of what you have already discovered about yourself. They may sometimes help if you are "stuck," as the assessment can be an icebreaker. It is important to realize that these tests do not give you answers. That is, they will not tell you what career to follow. But they provide information about your skills and interests, which helps you understand yourself and assists you in career decisions.

REFERENCES

Bolles, Richard. *What Color Is Your Parachute?* Berkeley: Ten Speed Press, annual.

Firestone, Robert W. *Compassionate Child Rearing.* New York: Plenum Press, 1990.

Holland, John L. *Understanding Yourself and Your Career.* Palo Alto, CA: Consulting Psychologists Press, 1977.

Kotter, John B., Victor A. Faux, and Charles McArthur. *Self-Assessment and Career Development.* Englewood Cliffs, NJ: Prentice-Hall, 1978.

Osipow, Samuel H. *Theories of Career Development.* 3d ed. Englewood Cliffs, NJ: Prentice-Hall, 1983.

Resources

for Finding Out about Exploring Careers by Looking within You

Fiction

Cormier, Robert. **The Chocolate War.** New York: Dell, 1974. 220p.

Cormier writes about a boys' school and the development of individuality. He explores the stress of growing up and describes the cruelty that occurs. This story is an illustration of the pressure to conform.

Santini, Rosemarie. **Ask Me What I Want.** New York: Fawcett, 1989. 133p.

A girl must choose between what she wants and what her mother wants for her. This is a story of an individual's conflicts in both career and personal matters.

Tan, Amy. **The Joy Luck Club.** New York: Ballantine, 1989. 322p.

Amy Tan's best-selling novel is a beautiful saga of four Chinese women and their lives in China, their subsequent American experiences, and the lives of their American-born daughters. These moving accounts illustrate mother-daughter relationships as well as cultural conflicts, and will help illuminate the experiences of many second-generation Americans. Conflicting career aspirations between parents and children is one of the diverse issues raised in this book.

Nonfiction

BOOKS

Baker, Russell. **Growing Up.** New York: Congdon and Weed, 1982. 278p.

The memoirs of the well-known *New York Times* columnist provide a moving perspective on the impact family values and attitudes in his formative years had on his life choices.

Bingham, Mindy. **Challenges: A Young Man's Journal for Self-Awareness and Personal Planning.** Santa Barbara: Advocacy Press, 1987. 239p.

This book deals with the myths and realities young men may face and provides assistance in areas of self-awareness and personal life planning.

Bingham, Mindy. **Choices: A Teen Woman's Journal for Self-Awareness and Personal Planning.** Updated. Santa Barbara: Advocacy Press, 1987. 240p.

The author addresses a range of the myths and realities a young woman is likely to face throughout her life. This book is useful in helping to understand and plan for personal and work-related choices.

Bolles, Richard. **What Color Is Your Parachute?** Berkeley: Ten Speed Press, annual. 448p.

An annual guide to discovering personal goals, skills, and areas of interest. Also provides tips on applying that information to obtaining employment. A comprehensive resource and easy to read, this book contains detailed exercises to guide readers and increase their confidence about job hunting.

Bradshaw, John. **Bradshaw on: The Family: A Revolutionary Way of Self-Discovery.** Deerfield Beach, FL: Health Communications, 1988. 240p.

This volume focuses on how the values and attitudes learned while growing up become part of each individual. Bradshaw discusses how negative attitudes can be addressed. This approach helps you gain awareness of yourself and how you were influenced by your family.

Campbell, David. **If You Don't Know Where You Are Going, You'll Probably End Up Somewhere Else.** Allen, TX: Tabor, 1990. 136p.

A book to help evaluate interests, abilities, motivations, education, family, experience, and health, and how to use the information to establish goals.

Feynman, Richard P. **"Surely You're Joking, Mr. Feynman!" Adventures of a Curious Character.** New York: W.W. Norton, 1989. 346p.

A delightful autobiography emerges through the unconventional method of conversations with a friend. Feynman, one of the world's greatest theoretical physicists and winner of the Nobel Prize in 1965, talks about his childhood through adult years. His interests and highly curious and investigative mind come through, from his 11-year-old construction of radios to his undying love of puzzles and anything unconventional and difficult to analyze.

Gale, Barry, and Linda Gale. **Discover What You're Best At.** New York: Simon and Schuster, 1982. 159p.

This workbook is built around the National Career Aptitude System, a program developed by the authors. Formalized tests assist in the identification of interests, aptitudes, and abilities. Also includes a section on career clusters and a directory of 1,000 careers.

Gawain, Shakti. **Living in the Light.** San Rafael, CA: New World Library, 1986. 192p.

A "New Age" book that focuses on self-improvement. Gawain gives clear explanations and practical guidance for anyone who wants to learn how to listen to and act on the inner self. The author guides you through a process of looking at old patterns and belief systems that have stifled your potential, and also discusses family influence and the world of work.

Loughary, John W., and Theresa M. Ripley. **Career and Life Planning Guide.** Chicago: Cambridge Books, 1988. 167p.

A guide to help you gain understanding of yourself and set goals for your future.

Marlin, Emily. **Genograms: Exploring Personality, Career, and Love Patterns You Inherit.** Chicago: Contemporary, 1989. 160p.

Marlin explains how to uncover inherited behavior, personality traits, and opinions. The author suggests that the family you come from strongly influences who you are. She provides techniques to help you with your exploration of yourself and your family.

Vedral, Joyce. **I Dare You: How To Get What You Want out of Life.** New York: Ballantine, 1989. 128p.

A self-help book designed to help you feel better about yourself and get more out of life.

ARTICLES

Green, Lee. **"Like Father Like Son."** *Los Angeles Times Magazine* (18 June 1989): 14–16.

An inspiring true story of Milt McColl, a football player for the Los Angeles Raiders, who followed exactly in the path of his father with a successful professional football career and a medical career. This article raises the question of how children are affected and influenced by their parents' interests and values.

White, W. **"Profiles: Sylvia Earle."** *The New Yorker* 65 (3 July 1989): 41–45.

Fascinating account of a woman who followed her instincts, values, and interests from early childhood and became a world-famous marine biologist.

Nonprint Materials

AUDIOVISUALS

The Breakfast Club
Type: VHS video
Length: 92 min.
Cost: Purchase $19.95
Source: MCA/Universal Home Video
        70 Universal City Plaza
        Universal City, CA 91608
        (818) 777-4300
Date: 1984

Five high school students spend a Saturday in detention thinking about life. A look at society and the variety of values that exist, this feature movie demonstrates how growing up in different families affects who you become.

Career Exploration
Type: VHS video
Length: 47 min.
Cost: Rental $75
Source: Sunburst Communications
        39 Washington Avenue
        Pleasantville, NY 10570-3498
Date: 1990

Explores career options and sets viewers on the path to satisfying careers by helping them match their interests, aptitudes, likes, dislikes, and personality types to compatible careers.

Career Planning Videotapes
Type: VHS video
Length: 6 videotapes, 15 min. each
Cost: Purchase $50 each
Source: Opportunities for Learning, Inc.
        Career Aids
        941 Hickory Lane
        P.O. Box 8103
        Mansfield, OH 44901-8103
        (800) 243-7116

These dramatizations follow three high school students as they cope with parental pressures and unrealistic ambitions when planning their futures. The series includes: *Who Am I?*; *What Am I Good At?*; *Studying an Occupation*; *The Big Picture*; *Get a Job*; and *It's Your Move*.

Soapbox with Tom Cottle: Parents and Teenagers

Type: VHS video
Length: 30 min.
Cost: Purchase $59.95
Source: PBS Video
             1320 Braddock Place
             Alexandria, VA 22314-1698
             (800) 424-7963
Date: 1987

This program shows what happens when channels of communication between parents and children break down. Teens explain how they feel when their parents do not understand them, and how they want their relationships with their parents to change.

Soapbox with Tom Cottle: When I Grow Up

Type: VHS video
Length: 30 min.
Cost: Purchase $59.95
Source: PBS Video
             1320 Braddock Place
             Alexandria, VA 22314-1698
             (800) 424-7963
Date: 1987

What are the forces shaping young people's dreams? Seven teenagers share their hopes and fears about the future in this program. Teenagers consider their goals, values, fantasies, and their best guesses at reality.

COMPUTER SOFTWARE

Intellimation. **Career Values Connection** and **CareerLink**
P.O. Box 1922, Santa Barbara, CA 93116-1922. (805) 968-2291.
$24.95. (Hard disk; minimum memory: 1 Mb; HyperCard 1.0.)

Two interactive Macintosh computer tools designed to help students and others in career exploration. *CareerLink* matches a job-seeker's aptitudes, interests, and temperament with work-trait requirements. *Career Values Connection* is useful in helping students to relate personal preferences and values to different career alternatives.

Opportunities for Learning, Inc. **Life and Career Planning Software.** 941 Hickory Lane, Dept. XG 467, P.O. Box 8103, Mansfield, OH 44901-8103. $79.95.

A software program, designed for both Apple and IBM-compatible computers, that helps students learn the importance of deciding what type of lifestyle to strive for and how their career goals affect the way they live. Situations are presented and students are asked to make decisions about their goals and lifestyle preferences. The program culminates with a printout of the student's long- and short-term goals. Includes one disk with backup and two copies of "Planning Your Future: What about Tomorrow?"

Services

Career Assessment Inventory
National Computer Systems
Box 1416
Minneapolis, MN 55440

An assessment for those who wish to enter a career immediately after high school or who want an occupation requiring technical or trade school, business school, or community college training. It is self-administered but computer-scored. You get a detailed printout of data and a narrative to help you gain insight into yourself and some occupations that may interest you.

Personal Skills Map
Institute for the Development of Human Resources
1202 Second Street
Corpus Christi, TX 78404

The Personal Skills Map guides the user to develop a "map" for personal and professional growth and change. This is particularly helpful if you are in the early stage of exploring potential occupations and educational directions.

SIGI PLUS
The Sigi Office
Educational Testing Service
Rosedale Road
Princeton, NJ 08541

A very useful program that guides you in assessing your values, interests, and skills. After the skills analysis and self-exploration, the program generates individualized lists of occupations, preparation requirements, occupational trend information, and salary ranges.

Strong-Campbell Interest Inventory
National Computer Systems
Box 1416
Minneapolis, MN 55440

This assessment tool was developed more than 50 years ago but has been updated to reflect new occupational areas. It is self-administered and computer-scored. The user receives a computer printout.

CHAPTER 3

Understanding Careers: Looking Ahead to the Twenty-First Century

This chapter talks a bit about the work world of the twenty-first century and some of the trends that will affect not only your career decisions, but also your daily work life once those decisions have been made.

The Rapid Pace of Change

It is clear that as we get closer to the year 2000, the workplace is being transformed so rapidly that an occupation you work at today may be completely changed tomorrow. Of course, it has not always been this way. Until quite recently, the pace of technological change was slow, and generations tended to overlap in the work world. For example, coal miners' sons often followed them into mining; it was not uncommon to find generations of steelworker grandfathers, fathers, and sons, especially in heavily industrialized areas such as Pennsylvania and West Virginia. If you learned an occupation when you were young, the chances were good you would earn your livelihood from it throughout your entire working life. Things are far different today.

What causes all this rapid change? Automation, for one thing. Here are some ways in which automation has already transformed our lives:

The scene: A health care office in a major North-eastern city. Patients come and go all day, but they see a live doctor or nurse only briefly. They have been checked in, registered, had their medical histories recorded, and even been administered routine tests by computers. The computer issues a preliminary diagnosis and an unsigned prescription for medication. Only at the completion of this automated process will the patient see the doctor.

The scene: Your living room during the busy holiday shopping season. You have decided not to fight the crowds at the mall and to do your shopping from your electronic catalogue instead. Your video screen displays pictures and information about a product you like. You phone your order in to a telemarketing center that checks the inventory, arranges for shipping and delivery, and electronically bills your credit card.

The scene: A large auto dealership in the Midwest. A family has just bought a new car. The sales clerk says, "You know, when you drive off in this car, yours will be the first human hands that have ever touched it, apart from the mechanics who test-drove it." The car was built entirely by robots.

These scenarios are already in place. And as technology continues to evolve, so will the workplace. In fact, many jobs we know today may completely disappear tomorrow, and others previously unheard of will appear.

Revolution in the Workplace: The Ever-Present Computer

Some people feel that the invention of the computer chip has had an impact comparable to that of the major inventions in history, such as the printing press, the cotton gin, the telephone, the steam engine, and even atomic energy. We already live in a world where the great majority of jobs involve the use of computers.

Take a look at a typical business operation such as a bank or an insurance company. It does not take long to realize that computers have moved in, taken over, and redefined the workplace. We now have machines that listen, speak, write, rewrite, correct spelling, store information, and even send out for their own repairpersons when they are broken!

Whatever your future career, it may well include working in an office setting at least part of the time. How will this work environment look? Try a little guessing game. Following the model of one of those trendy magazines, see if you can list the things that would make the magazine's Top Ten "in" (popular, fashionable) and "out" (old-fashioned, outmoded) lists. Here's ours:

IN	OUT
Interoffice electronic mail	Memos on paper
Computerized voice machines	Switchboard operator for telephone messages
Automatic spell check	Dictionary
Fax	Telegram
Car telephone	Messengers
Computer files	File cabinets

We could keep going, but you get the message.

Whether or not you are convinced that robots and computers will take over the workplace (and there certainly is controversy on this question, even among the "futurists"), you will not be surprised to learn that advancing technology ensures that "the information industry" is already having a major impact on the workplace.

Many experts predict that by the year 2000, most workers will be involved to some extent in operating, managing, or designing information systems such as computerized data bases, in a wide variety of occupations. Certainly, fields such as robotics, space, and energy, will provide many of the emerging careers by the end of this century.

While high-tech employment is a fast-growing section of the job market, it is also relatively small. In fact, only a very few of you can be expected to go into careers solely focused on technology, such as electronics, computer systems, or electrical engineering. But computers affect all industries and are changing even traditional occupations. Robots and computers may change how the job is done, but our society will always need many of the traditional occupations, such as teachers, nurses, accountants, carpenters, and salespeople.

Still, it is undeniable that the computer age is here! Computers issue cash at banks, check out groceries in the supermarket, and prepare and mail bills. Computers issue tickets for trains, planes, buses, theaters, and concerts. Paychecks are recorded and sent by computer. Every aspect of daily living is affected by computers.

What Does the Computer Revolution Mean to You?

In the early stages of thinking about careers and the skills and education that go along with them, you cannot help but feel bombarded by talk of the "computer revolution." You may even have felt that, unless you were a computer whiz focusing solely on technical and highly specialized skills, you would have few worthwhile career opportunities. Nothing could be further from the truth.

With all the emphasis on computers and high technology, we need to remember that in the early 1990s, only one out of eight workers use computers. And of these, only 5 percent need extensive computer training. The rest simply operate computers for specific purposes and learn the skills in a few hours or a few weeks, usually in on-the-job training.

While it is true that math, science, and computer skills will always be in great demand, they are simply part of a broad range of skills needed on any job. Rather than trying to be a computer expert, it makes more sense for you to focus on getting as good a general education as possible. It is the "generalist" skills, such as problem-solving, analyzing, and creative thinking, that will stand you in good stead, no matter what career you choose and how many times you move from one field to another. As John Sculley, the president of Apple Computer Company, pointed out in his examination of the global dynamic economy, computers are taking over the repetitive tasks of the workplace. With this type of work reduced or eliminated, more workers will be challenged with more important tasks: They will be expected to take part in critical decision making and to use broader problem-solving skills. The whole nature of work is being restructured by the computer.

You need only to look around you to realize immediately how rapidly the workplace is becoming computerized. Whether you are looking at fields as diverse as design, advertising, journalism, or sales, you will need to be comfortable around computers. If you are not "computer-literate," and at least able to do data entry, word processing, and graphics, it will be almost as hard for you to function in the world of work as if you were illiterate, that is, could not read or write.

Working in the Twenty-First Century

Although no one can say with certainty just what the future will be like, economists at the U.S. Department of Labor make it their business to study major trends and make predictions based on these trends. Experts at the Hudson Institute, a think tank specializing in forecasting the future, have gathered some valuable material that has clear implications for anyone making career plans and choices in the 1990s.

TREND ONE: MORE OLDER WORKERS

The work force is getting older. Already the pool of young people seeking jobs is shrinking. "Help Wanted" signs appear in places that traditionally employ young people, such as fast-food stores or companies offering part-time or seasonal employment. More people are living and working longer. Retirement commonly comes at age 70 or later, instead of the former age of 65.

What this means is that it may take longer for you to advance past entry-level and even mid-level positions. Older workers may remain longer in management and supervisory positions and you may feel "stuck" if promotions and advancement don't come as fast as you might wish. Rather than discouraging you, this situation could provide an incentive for you to get further training or learn new skills. You might even be motivated to change jobs or enter an entirely new field.

TREND TWO: MORE WOMEN ON THE JOB

In the prime-time television programs of the 1960s and 1970s, the "American family" was easily recognizable: Father went to work and Mother stayed home, cooking, cleaning, and taking care of the children and pets. Indeed, this picture was a pretty accurate reflection of those years when only about one-third of American women worked outside the home. Today the situation has changed dramatically. The Hudson Institute's statistics show this trend clearly: Women made up 33.4 percent of the work force in 1960, 42.5 percent in 1980, and are expected to constitute almost half or 47.5 percent by 2000.

Largely as a result of the greater numbers of women in the job market, gender barriers are slowing breaking down. Increasingly, fields that were previously closed unless you were male now offer attractive job prospects for both sexes. Certainly, women are benefiting from this trend and are exploring the ever-growing number of jobs and occupations that were once off limits to female candidates.

TREND THREE: MORE MINORITIES AND IMMIGRANTS IN THE WORK FORCE

Over the next few decades, African-Americans, Hispanics, Asians, and other minorities will make up a larger and larger share of the newcomers into the labor market. Bureau of Labor

Statistics figures show a growth in the number of minorities in the labor force from 11 percent in 1970 to 13.6 percent in 1985, and an estimated 15.5 percent by 2000. Perhaps more striking is that 29 percent of all new employees will be minorities.

Trends also indicate that the number of immigrants in the population and in the work force will increase in the next decade at a faster rate than at any time since early in the twentieth century. Beginning in the 1970s, new waves of immigration, primarily from Asia and Latin America, have been changing the face of many job markets in the United States, particularly in California, Texas, and New York.

These recent immigrants face many of the same obstacles as did the immigrants in earlier eras—language barriers, cultural differences, and prejudice. Of course, continued education and training are vitally important to those determined to break out of this rut.

TREND FOUR: MORE JOBS IN SERVICES AND INFORMATION

Plant layoffs in mining and factory closures in industries such as aerospace have become common in the past few years. The manufacturing industries that produce goods and products are slowing down. The demand for workers in agriculture, forestry, and fisheries is steadily decreasing.

In contrast, the service-producing industries will account for almost all the projected employment growth in the years ahead. Occupations in wholesale or retail trade, finance, insurance, and real estate are all expected to be in the high growth field. The Bureau of Labor Statistics expects more than ten million jobs to be added to service industries by the year 2000.

As you look at the choices and options open to you, you will want to keep these forecasts in mind. As a worker in tomorrow's world, you may well be employed in services such as health care or advertising, or marketing a business product rather than making the goods yourself. Certainly, projections of future job opportunities are important to consider in your career search.

TREND FIVE: MORE JOBS WILL REQUIRE
MORE EDUCATION

Looking at occupations as different as supermarket manager, hospital nurse, or financial analyst, it is clear that all workers will need higher levels of education in order to cope with the effects of changes in technology. Projections show a growth in the share of jobs requiring at least one year of college and a decline in the share of jobs requiring only a high school education.

Fast-growing occupations such as paralegals, medical assistants, physical therapists, all types of health-care aides, and computer processors and analysts will require increasing amounts of training and education. The job fields that are growing fastest demand higher skills in language, reasoning, and math than ever before. Especially for minorities and immigrants who have been concentrated in those jobs that today are declining or growing slowly, the message is clear: In order to be competitive and have a chance in the fast-growing fields, stay in school and get as good an education as you can.

REFERENCES

Aburdene, Patricia, and John Naisbitt. *Megatrends 2000: Ten New Directions for the 1990s*. New York: Avon, 1991.

Bureau of Labor Statistics. *Occupational Outlook Handbook, 1988–89*. Washington, DC: U.S. Government Printing Office, 1988.

Goldstein, H., and B. Fraser. "Computer Training and the Workplace: A Little Goes a Long Way." *Occupational Outlook Quarterly* 29 (Winter 1985): 24–29.

Hopkins, Kevin, and William B. Johnston. *Opportunity 2000*. Washington, DC: U.S. Government Printing Office, 1988.

Johnston, William B. *Workforce 2000*. Indianapolis: Hudson Institute, 1987.

McDaniels, Carl. *The Changing Workplace*. San Francisco: Jossey-Bass, 1989.

Reich, Robert B. "The Future of Work." *Harper's Magazine* (April 1989): 26–31.

Robertson, James. *FutureWork: Jobs, Self-Employment, and Leisure after the Industrial Age.* New York: Universe Books, 1985.

Sculley, John. "Forum on Human Investment." Speech given in Seattle, WA, 8 January 1991.

Wegmann, Robert G., Robert Chapman, and Miriam Johnson. *Work in the New Economy: Careers and Job-Seeking in the 21st Century.* Indianapolis: JIST Works, 1989.

Resources
for Finding Out about the
Twenty-First Century Workplace

Fiction

Asimov, Isaac. **Robot Dreams.** New York: Berkley Publishing Group, 1986. 349p.

The distinguished author is a scientist and weaves much scientific knowledge into these short stories. Topics include a space walk, computers, computerized automobiles, and robots that develop human characteristics. Other stories are scientific puzzles and extraterrestrial thrillers.

Ballard, J. G. **Memories of the Space Age.** Sauk City, WI: Arkham House, 1988. 216p.

A collection of eight stories presented against the backdrop of today's technological, space-age civilization: launch pads, satellites, and vaporized aluminum and ionized hydrogen peroxide gas from capsules in space. These powerful stories combine science, technology, and humanity and stress the psychological implications of space exploration.

Belden, Wilanne Schneider. **Mind-Hold.** New York: Harcourt Brace Jovanovich, 1987. 256p.

In the spirit of George Orwell and Aldous Huxley, this science fiction tale takes a journey through a not-too-distant future in a society in which behavior control is part of everyday life.

Cherryh, C.J. **Cyteen.** New York: Warner Books, 1988. 680p.

An intelligent science fiction novel that covers a full range of technological, political, social, and psychological changes in the world of tomorrow.

Colville, Bruce. **Space Station Ice-3.** New York: Scholastic, 1987. 188p.

Sixteen-year-old Rusty McPhee lives in a space colony with his parents. He gets involved in a murder mystery involving a dead body in a chemical waste–treatment plant. A timely issue presented in a fast-moving and absorbing story.

Huxley, Aldous. **Brave New World Revisited.** New York: Harper, 1958. 192p.

The author of a classic science fiction novel, originally written in 1932, takes a new look at it over 25 years later. The novel describes a world where automation has taken over and individuals are valued only as they contribute to the good of the whole. The political, ethical, and moral questions raised make this book relevant today.

Rochewald, Robert L. **Forward.** New York: Simon and Schuster, 1990. 470p.

A fascinating science fiction account of a group of brave scientists who staff the first expedition to Bernard's Star. They know they have been sent on a mission, never to return. This novel is solidly based on scientific fact, and gives a vivid portrayal of the lives of those who have chosen careers in space exploration and science.

Sagan, Carl. **Contact.** New York: Simon and Schuster, 1985. 398p.

A cryptic message from 26 light-years away reaches Earth, and Eleanor Arroway, a young, brilliant mathematician, is one of the primary decoders. The message reveals blueprints for a spacecraft. The book raises interesting questions about the changes that space travel will inevitably bring to humanity.

Streiber, Whitley, and James Kunetka. **Nature's End: The Consequences of the Twentieth Century.** New York: Warner Books, 1986. 418p.

Nuclear damage, hydrocarbon pollution, and overpopulation threaten the future of all the inhabitants of Earth. A group of concerned computer scientists struggle to expose the real motives of a newly elected president. The answers lie in coded computer files that destruct if incorrectly entered.

Nonfiction

BOOKS

Aburdene, Patricia, and John Naisbitt. **Megatrends 2000: Ten New Directions for the 1990s.** New York: Avon, 1991. 448p.

A lively and thought-provoking best-seller that describes social indicators and conditions, and makes predictions for the United States well into the next century.

Butler, Diane. **Futurework.** New York: Holt, Rinehart & Winston, 1984. 238p.

This book provides an introduction to the impact of computer technology on the world of work. The author discusses the implications of computers on jobs and careers. A good explanation is provided of such revolutionary inventions as the semiconductor, the transistor, and the microchip as they are transforming the modern work world.

Collard, Betsy A. **The High Tech Career Book.** Los Altos, CA: William Kaufmann, 1986. 300p.

A useful guide to the high-tech career world. This text can help you understand the ins and outs of the new jobs evolving in response to progress and technology. Special features include a glossary of industry terms, lists of professional associations, organizational charts, and a section on strategy planning.

Cornish, Edward, ed. **The 1990s and Beyond.** Bethesda, MD: World Future Society, 1990. 160p.

A thought-provoking look at the final decade of the twentieth century and the beginning of the twenty-first. Includes articles on artificial intelligence, medical breakthroughs, the earth's vital signs, tomorrow's economy, the future of AIDS, and much more.

Forsyth, Richard. **Machines That Think.** New York: Warwick Press/Science in Action, 1986. 37p.

A clear overview of what is meant by "expert systems" and "artificial intelligence." A program simulates a "guided search" strategy for a robot rat to find a route through a maze to some robot cheese.

O'Neill, Catherine. **Computers, Those Amazing Machines.** Washington, DC: National Geographic Society, 1985. 104p.

What do Michael Jackson, Olympic athletes, and General Motors have in common? Each uses the power of the computer to enhance special performance needs. This book captures the excitement of computers in action at home, school, workplace, sports, and entertainment. It provides a comprehensive view of the impact of computers on modern society and takes a peek at the possibilities for the future.

U.S. Department of Labor. **Career Guide to Professional Associations.** 2d ed. New York: Carroll Press, 1980. 260p.

This directory of organizations, compiled and edited by the staff of Carroll Press, is matched to the U.S. Department of Labor's *Directory of Occupational Titles.* It gives comprehensive information about each association, including address, phone, type of assistance provided, and information offered. A useful resource for following up on an occupation in which you are interested.

Winkler, Connie. **Careers in High Tech.** New York: ARCO, Prentice-Hall, 1987. 220p.

This volume looks at the broad spectrum of technologies and provides an overview of the world of the 1990s and beyond. You will learn about the job opportunities, growth potential, and challenges offered by many dynamic fields in high technology. Skills, training, and educational requirements are also provided for each field.

ARTICLES

Goldstein, H., and B. Fraser. **"Computer Training and the Workplace: A Little Goes a Long Way."** *Occupational Outlook Quarterly* 29 (Winter 1985): 24–29.

Based on a survey of 140 occupations carried out by the National Institute for Work and Learning, this article notes that only a small proportion of occupations require extensive computer training. It offers a useful checklist of occupations, especially if you are concerned about what computer training is and who requires it.

Kilborn, Peter T. **"Youths Lacking Special Skills Find Jobs Leading Nowhere."** *New York Times* (27 November 1990).

First part of a three-part series of articles titled "Scraping By," which focuses on the changes in the job market and the need for young people to pursue as much schooling as possible. Some graphic statistics show how young workers fall behind when the economy is in a downturn. The emphasis is on the need to prepare young people for high-quality, better-paying jobs by improving the quality of the schooling they receive.

Walsh, Darrel Patrick. **"Artificial Intelligence."** *Occupational Outlook Quarterly* 33, no. 2 (Summer 1989): 2–7.

Making a machine seem intelligent is not easy. As a consequence, demand has been rising for computer professionals skilled in artificial intelligence, and it is likely to go up. These workers develop expert systems and solve the mysteries of machine vision, natural language processing, and neural networks.

Nonprint Materials

America by Design: The Workplace
Type: VHS video
Length: 60 min.
Cost: Purchase $79.95
Source: PBS Video
           1320 Braddock Place
           Alexandria, VA 22314-1698
           (800) 424-7963
Date: 1987

Traces the evolution of the workplace from mills to factories to office towers, and conveys the status and success these facilities represent in our society.

Computer Careers
Type: VHS video
Length: 28¹/₂ min.
Cost: Rental $75; purchase $195
Source: AIMS Media
           6901 Woodley Avenue
           Van Nuys, CA 91406-4878
           (800) 367-2467
Date: 1987

Learning about computers is now essential for many jobs. This video looks at traditional occupations that require some degree of computer literacy, including manufacturers, designers, doctors, dentists, lawyers, teachers, etc. Computer industry careers are also described—each job is defined, and the educational requirements are provided.

One Small Step
Type: VHS video
Length: 25 min.
Cost: Purchase $295

Source: The Media Guild
              Sorrento Valley Road
              San Diego, CA 92121

Date: 1989

How are computer systems designed to be reliable? What types of jobs are available that use computers? These are some of the questions answered within the framework of the National Aeronautics and Space Administration (NASA) Shuttle Program. Engineers are shown solving problems and engaged in the teamwork that goes into making complex systems operate.

CHAPTER 4

Career Awareness: Figuring It All Out

No doubt there are times when the world of careers and the process of career planning seem like a maze to you. At those times you may despair of finding a clear path through to the end, but take heart. It won't be easy but it can be done. When you consider that your career and job choices in the years ahead are among the most important decisions you will make throughout your life, it is not surprising that a degree of agony and pain accompanies this process.

You can expect to spend a tremendous number of your waking hours at work. Therefore, it is certainly worth the extra time and effort to find a career or job that feels right for you—one that meets your needs and allows you to express your beliefs and goals, exert your creativity, and feel satisfied, at least most of the time. The additional energy and effort you put into the career-planning process will be well worth it if they help you achieve this goal.

In many ways the entire career-search process can be reduced to some basic, simple questions: What do you want out of a career? What's out there? How do you make the choices? How do you get there? What do you do when you arrive?

Describing the Most Important Person in Your Life: You

This exercise asks you to pretend that you are applying for a very special job. This task is unique because, on the basis of a profile of yourself that you provide, the employer will create the job that best suits you! In the real world, of course, you would have to show that you could fit into some existing job. But in our exercise, the job will be created to fit you.

Of course, you should be as honest about yourself as possible. Everyone's profile will be different, but, as you write this short essay, you might find it useful to try to cover some of the following points:

YOUR PROFILE

1. *Your work life (real or imagined):* Describe your job day, how intense your work is, whether you work with people or on your own, aspects of the job you like most, aspects you dislike most, how well you carry out responsibilities, how you respond to stress.
2. *Your personal life:* Your energy level, your likes and dislikes, what you do to relax, how you work off steam, what you do for physical exercise, how you describe your health.
3. *Your interests and abilities:* What you are good at doing, what your strongest talents are, in what things you have been most successful. Identify some people you know who are working in really interesting or challenging jobs. What sounds best: working with numbers? with your hands? alone? with people?

Writing Your Own Job Description

Suppose you were given the opportunity to create your ideal job. If you have given ample thought to the exercises on the previous pages and you have a good understanding of your values and goals, then you are ready to develop a scenario about how you would most like to spend your future. It may be helpful to look back at your answers to the personal inventory exercises in Chapter 2 in order to keep your interests, abilities, needs, and preferences in mind. Remember to be both realistic and imaginative. You want to give yourself the broadest range of possibilities!

YOUR IDEAL JOB DESCRIPTION

1. Job title: What do you do? What is the nature of your work?
2. Whom do you work for? Are you self-employed? Or are you part of an organization? Do you work alone or as part of a team?
3. What are your overall goals and responsibilities; your day-to-day tasks? Do you have a chance to be creative?
4. What is your salary? How much vacation time is available? Are there travel requirements? What fringe benefits go along with this job?

Don't get discouraged by the amount of thought, energy, and time it takes to write this ideal job description or to do the other self-assessment exercises. In the long run, all the effort you put in now will pay off many times over.

What's out There? How Do You Choose?

It is pretty scary to realize how many thousands of different kinds of occupations exist. A person could get dizzy just thinking about all the possibilities. Even if you have narrowed the list to the general fields in which you are interested, there are still so many occupations and directions in which one could go that the prospect might seem daunting.

Without an idea of where you're going, of course, it doesn't matter much how you get there. And in order to know where you're going, you need a good sense of the different types of occupations so that you can be thinking about which ones sound appealing. One way to approach this is to think in terms of the academic subjects that have interested you in school and in which you have done well. Of course, you may actually go in a different direction but it is a useful first step to think about your strengths and current interests.

Let's begin with those subjects that cluster under science and math: biology, chemistry, physics, and mathematics. If you have enjoyed these subjects, you are probably analytical and inquisitive, and you enjoy experimenting and questioning. You like to work with animals and plants (biology), or to figure out the makeup of all the elements that surround us (chemistry), or to understand the laws of math and physics that govern the world (physics). Below is just a handful of the occupations into which each of these subjects might lead you.

BIOLOGY

Zoologist

Anthropologist

Botanist

Physician

Veterinarian

Forester

CHEMISTRY

Bacteriologist

Chemical engineer

Laboratory technician

Dietician

Pharmacist

Metallurgist

Geologist

PHYSICS

Electronics engineer

Nuclear physicist

Meteorologist

Electrician

Aeronautical engineer

Ophthalmologist

MATHEMATICS

Bookkeeper

Accountant

Banker

Insurance broker

Statistician

Navigator

Another set of subjects cluster in the creative fields or the arts (art, drama, music, dance). You may have a special talent that you have been cultivating through extracurricular and in-school activities. There are obvious arts careers such as pianist, painter, sculptor, or actress. These are all highly glamorous for the few who are successful. But perhaps you had not thought of other careers related to the arts fields, such as:

THE ARTS

Advertising

Architect

Draftsperson

Interior decorator

Stage designer

Occupational therapist

Instrument repairperson

Producer

Composer

English and foreign languages create another cluster of academic skills and interests. An aptitude in these fields is excellent preparation for just about every career that involves writing, research, or any of the communication skills. But some careers have a particularly close relation to these fields. A few of these are:

ENGLISH

Teacher

Lawyer

Journalist

FOREIGN LANGUAGES

Librarian

Travel agent

Translator

Radio, TV announcer

Foreign Service officer

FBI agent

Still another career cluster focuses around the social sciences. While these fields cover a wide range, the high school subjects most closely related are social studies, government, history, psychology, and health education. There are many interesting careers to explore if you have an interest and ability in any of these fields:

SOCIAL SCIENCES

Anthropologist

Social worker

Lawyer

Sociologist

Economist

Political scientist

Public-health nurse

Clinical psychologist

Finally, the area of business education attracts people who enjoy working with numbers and computers and who like the world of business with all its diverse opportunities. Industrial arts appeals to those who enjoy shop and mechanical courses, like working with their hands, and possess skill and patience in a particular craft. Here are just a few of the many possible occupations:

BUSINESS EDUCATION

Advertising executive

Salesperson

Manager

Word-processing specialist

Accountant

Stockbroker

Banker

Beautician

Nutritionist

INDUSTRIAL ARTS

Carpenter

Plumber

Mechanic

Electrician

Engineer

Landscape architect

Draftsperson

How Do You Get There? Doing Your Research

If you are still somewhat unclear about your sense of direction, you may wish to take some further tests on vocational interests, abilities, and temperament, and to talk at length with a career counselor at your school. Once your sights are clearer, you are ready for the next step: library research.

While you may associate the library only with required schoolwork, this is not at all the case. Your local library is an excellent place to continue your career research. Almost all libraries have books, magazines, and pamphlets about the world of work. Talk to the reference librarian; your library probably has a "careers" section and the librarian will be able to assist you to make the best use of the card catalogue and computer resources.

SOME FIRST STEPS: USING THE LIBRARY

1. Spend some time with the *Occupational Outlook Handbook* available in the reference section of any library. Look through the table of contents and pick out three broad career areas, such as "service occupations" or "mechanics and technicians." Jot down the jobs in these categories that appeal to you. Keep track of the *Dictionary of Occupational Titles* (DOT) number next to the job title.

2. Look up these job titles by their numbers in the DOT and read their descriptions. Similar DOT numbers are clues to related jobs. Also look at the alphabetical index of job titles in the back of the DOT.

3. The *Guide for Occupational Exploration* (GOE) is another useful reference book. Look up a job in which you're interested. Read about the skills, education, duties, and responsibilities the job calls for. Let's say you are interested in biology or chemistry. Look up "biologist" and "chemist" in the index; get their numbers, then look them up in the "Scientific: Life Sciences" section.

4. Finally, for each job in which you are interested, write the DOT number and the job title on a separate page in your careers notebook. Using all the references listed in steps 1–3, answer these questions:

   What does a person with this job title do?

   What kinds of skills are required?

How much education is required?

What is the job outlook for the future?

What is the salary range?

What are some related occupations?

What skills need to be developed?

What experience or training is needed?

After you have answered these questions for three jobs or careers, go back and look at your earlier inventories of values, skills, and interests (see Chapter 2). How well do your answers to the questions about specific jobs match those in your inventories? It's also important to read about people in these careers. Biographies, autobiographies, novels, and movies are all interesting and useful ways to get a personal feel for what a particular career is like.

Finally, try to get as much firsthand information as possible. Talk to as many people who hold these jobs as you can. Your own common sense will tell you the kinds of questions to ask. In general, you want to find out how they decided to do what they are doing, what they like best, what they like least, and whether or not they'd advise someone like you to consider that career. Career counselors call this informational interviewing. (See Chapter 7.)

Where To Get Help: Career-Resource Centers

Many schools, public libraries, community centers, colleges, and universities offer some type of resource center designed to provide information and assistance in career planning. If such a center is accessible, check it out. You may wish to talk to a career counselor who may be able to help you sharpen your career ideas and goals. Career centers are sometimes located in community organization centers such as YMCAs.

Although these centers vary in nature, most have collections of up-to-date print and nonprint career information. You can explore options, financial aid, placement and job finding, self-assessment, courses of study, and other reference materials.

Many career centers are staffed by professionals who are happy to assist you in using the information. Some centers offer seminars conducted by speakers in various careers or resource directories of people in the community who are willing to talk individually about their occupations. And many centers are able to refer you to useful work-experience programs.

There are hundreds of publications, directories, bibliographies, and other references that provide information on everything from correspondence courses to international jobs or financial aid opportunities to colleges and universities. Increasingly, these information sources are available in the form of audio or videotapes and computer software programs. See the end of this chapter for examples of career-information resources. They include:

1. *Standard references:* Encyclopedias of careers sometimes describe as many as 650 different occupations. Even more valuable are the occupational outlook handbooks that summarize most types of jobs and occupations and then group them into categories. These handbooks often provide useful projections on job trends and forecasts. Thumbing through some of these directories may be a good way to begin, as soon as you have some ideas of specific jobs that interest you.

2. *Specialized directories:* You may be interested in learning more about jobs with foreign travel and other international opportunities. Information is available on study-abroad programs at colleges and universities. A large number of exchange and study programs are also available for high school students. Other resources feature occupations that provide overseas travel or extended stays abroad.

3. *Directories of colleges and technical schools:* Since so many occupations require college degrees or at least several years of schooling beyond high school, you will find it helpful to consult these directories for names of schools that offer the programs in the fields that interest you. Additionally, there are good directories offering useful information on scholarships and financial aid.

4. Information from professional and trade associations, labor unions, and government: These materials are designed to attract you to specific professions or trades. As such, the information offered may be somewhat biased. Nonetheless, these materials are often useful, providing specific details on the profession or trade, including up-to-date trends, geographic factors, and salary information.

5. Computer-based career-information systems: If you are lucky enough to have access to a career-resource center, you will undoubtedly find a great deal of computer-based information. Computer programs allow you to input your biographical information and obtain up-to-date occupational matches. Often this information is cross-referenced with other source materials such as career kits, job-description cards, and audiovisual materials. Computers are able to provide current job information as well as assistance in resume writing, job interviewing, and other aspects of job placement.

What Do You Do When You Arrive? Myths and Realities

Career research and exploration are useful because they help dispel misleading or inaccurate information about different jobs or careers. Sadly, many young people make career choices based on myths and stereotypes rather than on accurate and adequate information. High-profile, glamorous professions such as those in television or theater, for example, attract people who have no idea of the drudgery and hard work that go on for years and years as the career is built. And they may be even less aware of the tiny number who really succeed. In a conversation with the author, Sally Rothberg, a television actress, describes her struggle in the early years of her career:

I was like an apprentice for my first year. You rehearse one show in the afternoon, perform another show in the evening, a children's show on the weekend, and a cabaret after the Saturday night show. It's a great training ground to see how much the body can actually withstand without sleep.

Salary? Forget it! The first year I had to *pay* $125 a week for the pleasure of working as an apprentice. In my second year I finally got paid.

The process of career research and exploration is different for each person and each field. But the more resources you consult—people, books, computer materials, films, reference books, etc.—the more thorough you will be. The job world is so dynamic and complex that the more you know about it, the better you will be prepared to cope with its changes and complexities.

REFERENCES

Carey, Max L. "Characteristics of Occupational Entrants." *Occupational Outlook Quarterly* 33, no. 2 (Summer 1989): 8–12.

Fowler, Elizabeth M. *The New York Times Career Planner.* New York: Times Books, 1987.

Haponski, William C., and Charles McCabe. *New Horizons.* Princeton, NJ: Peterson's Guides, 1985.

Phifer, Paul. *College Majors and Careers: A Resource Guide for Effective Life Planning.* Garrett Park, MD: Garrett Park Press, 1987.

U.S. Department of Labor. *Occupational Outlook Handbook.* Washington, DC: National Textbook, 1990.

Resources

for Finding Out about Building Your Career Awareness

Fiction

Becker, Stephen. **The Blue-Eyed Shan.** New York: Random House, 1982. 384p.

Before World War II, an American anthropologist is studying the Shan people in a tiny village on the border between China and Burma. Years later he is faced with a conflict regarding an earthshaking discovery of the bones of Peking Man in the village. This novel effectively illustrates the life and ethical dilemmas of an anthropologist facing competing loyalties to his friends in the village and the demands of his profession.

Benfor, Gregor. **Artifact.** New York: TOR Books, 1985. 533p.

On a routine archaeological dig in Greece, Claire Anderson uncovers a mysterious granite cube with an amber cone protruding from one side. Studying the artifact becomes increasingly difficult, however, when her strange Greek colleague jealously guards the find. A lively tale illustrating the mysteries and excitement an archaeologist can encounter.

Hurford, Daphne. **The Right Moves: A Dancer's Training.** New York: Atlantic Monthly Press, 1987. 238p.

This account of Max's struggles at the School of American Ballet shows how exhausting, both physically and emotionally, this profession can be. Although he is always in danger of pain and injury, Max is exhilarated at the idea of following in

the footsteps of great dancers like Peter Martins, Mikhail Bar-
ishnikov, and Rudolf Nureyev. The story shows the total commitment that ballet demands.

Ravin, Neil. **Evidence.** New York: St. Martin's Press, 1987.
292p.

A new chief of surgery is brought into St. George's Hospital.
Before long, many on the staff are grumbling about the unortho-
dox ways cases are being handled and the many complications
that result. This novel about doctors policing themselves gives
an interesting behind-the-scenes look at the hospital world and
will interest those considering a medical career. Prospective
lawyers will also enjoy its legal action and courtroom drama.

Sweeney, Joyce. **Right behind the Rain.** New York: Delacorte,
1987. 150p.

Carla's older brother shares his dreams and career aspirations
with her. He wants to be a movie actor, now that he has graduated
from college, and Carla gets caught up in his mood swings. The
book illustrates the struggles and the joys of an artistic career.

Nonfiction

BOOKS

America's Top 300 Jobs: A Complete Career Handbook.
Indianapolis: JIST Works, 1990. 450p.

Based on the U.S. Department of Labor's *Occupational Outlook Handbook*, this book contains readable and up-to-date
information. It will be especially useful to someone in the
beginning of career exploration because it offers information
on which careers and jobs are most interesting and how to
prepare for them. Each listing of an occupation includes the
nature of the work, working conditions, training, job outlook,
and sources of additional information.

Asimov, Isaac, and Frank White. **Space: Where Have We Been?
Where Are We Going?** New York: Walker, 1989. 120p.

This book does an excellent job of putting space exploration into perspective for young adults. Chapters trace the development of ideas about space and space travel, the dawn of the space age, and issues of space exploration today and in the future. Political and scientific issues are raised, and the United States' and the U.S.S.R.'s successes and failures are compared and contrasted. A "must" for anyone aspiring to a career in either science or politics.

Barbera-Hogan, Mary. **Straight Talk on Careers: 80 Pros Take You into Their Professions.** Garrett Park, MD: Garrett Park Press, 1987. 249p.

A leading lawyer, a computer systems analyst, a top motion-picture director, an army tank commander, a professional football quarterback, an elementary schoolteacher, and a state highway-patrol officer share their daily routines and the things they like and do not like about their jobs.

Bishop, John M. **Making It in Video: An Insider's Guide to Careers in the Fastest Growing Industry of the Decade.** New York: McGraw-Hill, 1989. 195p.

An introductory history of the industry precedes an informative discussion of videos for broadcast (commercial, public, and cable television), industrial, educational, and consumer use. The book includes profiles of individuals working in different areas of video, gives tips on pursuing a job or career, and looks at satisfaction desired.

Cvancara, Alan M. **Sleuthing Fossils: The Art of Investigating Past Life.** New York: Wiley, 1990. 203p.

This book is well suited for someone considering a career in the science of ancient life. Its well-written chapters are full of information, personal experiences, and descriptions of the work of several well-known paleontologists. It includes good lists of recommended readings.

Exploring Careers. Rev. 1990–1991 ed. Indianapolis: JIST Work, 1990.

This supplement to the U.S. Department of Labor's *Occupational Outlook Handbook* is compiled by the staff of JIST

Works. The first section helps you match your skills and interests with possible careers. Each job cluster section begins with interviews of someone who works in that field.

Franck, Irene M., and David M. Brownstone. **Scientists and Technologists.** New York: Facts on File, 1988. 212p.

Focuses on those occupations associated with scientific research and technology, including astrologers, astronomers, biologists, computer scientists, engineers, geologists, mathematicians, physicists, and statisticians. A handy reference source written in clear and simple language, this book explains how and why occupations evolved throughout history.

Harkaway, J. **101 Careers: A Guide to the Fastest Growing Opportunities.** New York: Wiley, 1990. 352p.

Information on top jobs for the 1990s. This guide provides an overview of major occupations: accounting, finance, banking, sales, marketing, engineering, computer science, social sciences, education, health care, entertainment, media, and more. It also includes addresses of associations, information on trade and professional journals, and resume and interview tips.

Lovell, Bernard L. **Astronomer by Chance.** New York: Basic, 1990. 381p.

What is a career in science like? The autobiography of a scientist can provide an answer. Lovell's career was delightfully unpredictable, and his account of his childhood spent building radio sets instead of doing schoolwork will interest anyone. His career switches, from mathematics to radar research to astronomy, make a fascinating tale and a useful one if you are considering a career in any of the sciences.

McAdam, Terry. **Doing Well by Doing Good: The First Complete Guide to Careers in the Nonprofit Sector.** New York: Penguin, 1986. 199p.

Clear, constructive information on all the aspects of working in the nonprofit sector makes this an essential guide to the many opportunities for careers in the helping professions.

Norback, Craig T., ed. **VGM's Careers Encyclopedia.**
Lincolnwood, IL: National Textbook, 1989. 484p.

A concise, up-to-date reference useful for students, parents, and guidance counselors. It provides detailed descriptions of more than 180 careers, listed alphabetically for quick reference. Each listing includes the responsibilities of the job, qualifications, education and training, potential advancement, and income.

Opportunities in . . .
Career Aids
Opportunties for Learning, Inc.
941 Hickory Lane
P.O. Box 8103
Mansfield, OH 44901-8103
(800) 243-7116

A definitive series of softcover books providing professional career guidance from recognized experts to help young adults choose and plan their future work. Discusses education, opportunities, earnings, potential for employment, and many other subjects. Includes 70 titles ranging from "Accounting" to "Word Processing."

Rosen Publishing Company issues a series of books on careers ranging from advertising to word processing. Each book talks about the kind of person who might be good in a certain career, the education needed to pursue it, and the job opportunities. The 1990 titles cover careers in aviation, banking and finance, fashion retailing, foreign languages, word processing and desktop publishing, professional sports, law enforcement and security, and computer sales. For information, call (800) 237-9932.

Sacharov, Al. **Offbeat Careers: The Directory of Unusual Work.** Berkeley: Ten Speed Press, 1988. 178p.

From acupuncturist to yacht crew member, here are 90 unusual work situations for the adventurous career explorer. For each occupation the author lists the basic job description, typical salaries, and essential education. The book includes references to associations and organizations for additional information.

Schefter, James L. **Telecommunications Careers.** New York: Franklin Watts, 1988. 112p.

This volume is one of a series on high-tech jobs, the fastest-growing career area in the nation. It provides a clear overview of this rising industry, with definitions of terms and explanations of the wide variety of career options and educational and training requirements. Topics covered include manufacturing, installation and operators, military uses, data and video communications.

Schmolling, Paul, et al. **Careers in Mental Health: A Guide to the Helping Occupations.** Garrett Park, MD: Garrett Park Press, 1986. 111p.

Designed for the young adult, this book focuses on a number of careers that involve helping people who have emotional problems. It covers ten major professions in the mental health field that require a range of educational backgrounds from high school to the doctoral level. It describes work settings, presents a series on "a day in the life of" various workers, and gives much other useful information.

Smith, Devon, ed. **The Fourth of July Resource Guide.** Garrett Park, MD: Garrett Park Press, 1987. 605p.

A useful overview of the great variety of careers found in public, community, and international service.

VGM Career Horizons. Lincolnwood, IL: National Textbook, 1987.

This company publishes an extensive series of reference books (each about 150 pages) outlining opportunities in more than 100 careers. Each book is written by a leading authority in the field, and covers many career options. They include organizations to contact, books to read, and schools to attend. Recent titles cover career opportunities in automotive services, office occupations, retailing, public health, laser technology, civil engineering, veterinary medicine, vocational and technical fields, paralegal and law enforcement, recreation, biological sciences, and pharmacy.

ARTICLE

Davis, Shelley J. **"The 1990–91 Job Outlook in Brief."** *Occupational Outlook Quarterly* 34, no. 1 (Spring 1990): 8–45.

A detailed account of how employment in 250 occupations is expected to change between 1988 and 2000. Occupations are grouped in 12 clusters such as executive, administrative, and managerial; technicians; marketing and sales; service; agriculture; forestry and fishing, etc.

MAGAZINE

Real World
King Features Syndicate
235 E. 45th Street
New York, NY 10017
Monthly. $15

A tabloid-sized 12-page monthly, this magazine of career information provides "a look ahead at life and work." A wide range of occupations is presented in each issue, and articles discuss responsibilities, qualifications, salaries and wages, plus the joys and difficulties of certain jobs. Addresses for further information are also included. A useful way to keep current on the career world.

Nonprint Materials

Broadcast News
Type:	VHS video
Length:	104 min.
Cost:	Standard rental charge
Source:	Regular video outlets
Date:	1987

A behind-the-scenes look at a television network news operation. This revealing feature film shows the pluses and minuses of a career in television news.

Career Aids
Opportunities for Learning, Inc.
941 Hickory Lane
P.O. Box 8103
Mansfield, OH 44901-8103

The Career Aids division of Opportunities for Learning stocks a large multimedia collection that will enhance any school- or community-based career center with videos, computer software, board games, and books on such topics as career planning, self-assessment resumes, and job hunting skills.

Common Threads: Stories from the Quilt
Type: VHS video
Length: 80 min.
Cost: Rental $150
Source: Direct Cinema, Ltd.
            P.O. Box 69799
            Los Angeles, CA 90069
Date: 1989

This award-winning film provides a gripping look at the impact of AIDS in the United States, covering both its history and especially the personal and family stories of its victims. This is a powerful film for anyone considering a career in science or medical research, and vitally important for anyone interested in the helping professions.

Icewalk
Type: VHS video
Length: 4 videos, 22–24 min. each
Cost: Rental $150 for the set
Source: PBS Video
            1320 Braddock Place
            Alexandria, VA 22314-1698
            (800) 424-7963
Date: 1990

The Icewalk school kit invites students and teachers to accompany an international expedition on its environmental research trek to the North Pole. Viewers experience frigid windchill temperatures, screaming winds, and frostbite firsthand as the explorers collect scientific data about our fragile environment. The kit includes four videos (*How Fragile These Frozen Seas; The Storm of Acid Snow; The Amazing Vanishing Ozone;* and *A Habitat Turned Hothouse*) and a teacher's guide. A good way to get a feeling for environmental science and wilderness research as career possibilities.

Planet Earth

Type: VHS video
Length: 7 episodes, 60 min. each
Cost: Rental free
Source: The Annenberg/CPB Collection
            1111 16th Street NW
            Washington, DC 20036
            (800) LEARNER

A comprehensive account of various environmental issues relating to the earth's water resources, forests, mountains, and valleys. This video provides good food for thought for those considering an environmentally related career.

The Right Stuff

Type: VHS video
Length: 106 min.
Cost: Standard rental charge
Source: Regular video outlets
Date: 1988

Based on the best-selling book of the same title by Tom Wolfe, this feature film presents the epic true story of the first seven astronauts chosen to launch the United States into space. This vivid fact-filled account of the behind-the-scenes hard work involved in space exploration will prove stimulating and thought-provoking for anyone considering an aeronautical or space-science career.

Stand and Deliver
Type: VHS video
Length: 106 min.
Cost: Standard rental charge
Source: Regular video outlets
Date: 1988

The uplifting story of the impact a charismatic and dedicated teacher has on the lives of his students. Set in East Los Angeles and based on the true story of Jaime Escalante, this feature film shows that minority youngsters can be high achievers if someone believes in them and motivates them. This film is highly inspirational for anyone thinking of teaching as a career.

That Teen Show: Career Opportunities of the Future
Type: VHS video
Length: 27 min.
Cost: Not available
Source: Saturn Productions, Inc.
             1697 Broadway
             Suite 1102
             New York, NY 10019
Date: 1989

Robert Marshall, director of program development at NASA's Marshall Space Flight Centers, discusses future job opportunities in space science.

The Truth about Teachers
Type: VHS video
Length: 45 min.
Cost: Rental $49.95
Source: Pyramid Film and Video
             Box 1048
             Santa Monica, CA 90406
Date: 1989

This program, hosted by film star Whoopi Goldberg, provides a vivid and stimulating view of ten exemplary teachers as they interact with their students. Situations span the spectrum from kindergarten to high school, special students to the gifted, the inner city to Appalachia, math and science to the performing arts.

CHAPTER 5

Traditional Career Preparation: Going to College

More School? When Is Enough Enough?

There are big decisions facing you after high school. Perhaps the biggest is the question of whether or not to get more education and training, and if so, whether to go to college. By now you should have a fairly good sense of some careers that seem both interesting and appropriate to your skills. You have thought about who you are and where you are heading. You have done some homework to figure out your skills, interests, and abilities, and you have talked to lots of people. Perhaps you have even tried some temporary or part-time employment in a field that interests you.

Now you face the decision about whether to pursue an education beyond high school and, if so, what type and how much. The reality is that today's job world is becoming specialized and technical, and qualifications are stiffening all the time. Because of this, you will probably want to give serious thought to some type of post–high school education. Higher education gives you new options, increases your earning capacity, brings you into contact with people at higher levels of responsibility, and certainly aids in your personal growth.

Higher-education programs vary a lot. This chapter discusses traditional programs, and the next chapter focuses on nontraditional types of post–high school education and training programs. Traditional programs are generally offered on either a two-year or a four-year college campus and take place in classrooms with instructors. More than 3,000 licensed or accredited colleges and universities exist in the United States and Canada. You can find small colleges with several hundred students, and huge universities that have thousands of students enrolled. Additionally, as we will see in Chapter 6, there are many trade and technical schools, business schools, and schools specializing in every kind of career from paralegal to cosmetology programs.

Once you have made your career choice and researched its educational requirements, you are ready for the next step: deciding which route is best for you to prepare for that career.

Four-Year Colleges and Universities

Many teenagers who graduate from high school today enroll in college. Four years of college is a big commitment and a major investment of your time and money. Think about the reasons why you want to go to college and be as honest with yourself as possible. Here are some reasons teenagers sometimes give. How many apply to you?

I want to get away from home.

I want to meet new people.

I want to learn more about a subject that interests me.

I don't want to disappoint my parents.

I want to prepare for a particular career.

All my friends are going; I don't want to be left behind.

I want to understand the world in which I live.

I want a general liberal arts education.

I want to put off the time when I have to get a job.

Sound familiar? Knowing which of these reasons applies to you will help you decide what to look for in a college. There are many excellent college guides (some are listed at the end of this chapter), and of course, you can get help from your advising office at school.

Although you may be eager to escape the constraints of school, you may well find college a very different experience from high school. You likely will meet people from a wide variety of backgrounds and have the chance to explore the challenges of the academic world. You will be exposed to many disciplines and opportunities that are rarely offered at the high school level; for example, you may choose to delve into archaeology, anthropology, and psychology, or to study a foreign language such as Russian or Chinese. You will also have the chance to set many of your own goals and work under your own direction.

The college years are a valuable time for you to discover career opportunities that you may not have known existed, or to clarify career goals that you set long ago. It is also a time to discover your preferred working style and to get experience in making your own decisions and choices. The next decade of your life will be a time of tremendous change, and your perspectives on life and work may evolve in new and unpredictable directions.

One of the things to decide early in your college career is whether to pursue a liberal arts education or to move immediately into a more technical or specialized area. Defining "the liberal arts" is not a simple undertaking. Perhaps it is easiest to think of it as a form of study that leads to a broad-based, general understanding of the roots of our civilization, as gleaned through literature, history, the arts, and sciences. In contrast, a specialized education prepares one for more narrowly defined professional and technical career goals, such as medicine or business.

Whatever your primary motives are at this time, you should not underestimate the importance of a strong liberal arts education for your career. A grounding in the liberal arts, particularly at the undergraduate level, will strengthen the verbal and analytical skills you bring to any discipline. And the more you know about the humanities and the social and natural sciences, the more informed career choices you can make in the future. A liberal arts undergraduate major such as history, English, philosophy, or one of the sciences makes sense. Should you then decide you want to go into a profession such as engineering, law, or social work, you will be in a good position to pursue additional specialized graduate training.

Community and Junior Colleges

If your career choice does not require a four-year college education, you may wish to consider one of the several thousand two-year schools. They are generally smaller and less costly than four-year institutions.

A two-year college may offer both transfer and terminal programs. Transfer programs let you receive an associate degree and transfer to an upper-division program at a four-year college or university. In this way, you have some extra years to get used to a college experience before taking on the financial and academic pressures of a four-year college. Generally, community college admission requirements are more flexible than those at four-year institutions, so even if you did not do well in high school you have a chance to enroll and succeed when you are older and better prepared mentally to do the work.

At the community college you can also enroll for a terminal degree, which prepares you for many occupations that require two years or less of full-time study. Normally these programs are technical and do not include the breadth of liberal arts material found in a four-year program. These kinds of degrees open up jobs in fields such as accounting, law enforcement, data processing, and dental hygiene. Many classes are held at night, so students are able to hold full-time jobs during the day, further keeping costs down.

Is Vocational Education for You?

If you have decided on an occupation that calls for specialized skills or talents, you may be a candidate for a trade or technical school (also see Chapter 6). These range from business colleges to beauty-culture institutes to programs for electricians and mechanics. In these programs, you can learn a specialized skill or trade in a relatively short time.

Do You Need a Special Program?

Perhaps you might benefit from a program that gives certain individuals and groups specialized attention. For instance, the Educational Opportunity Program (EOP) has an excellent reputation for providing assistance to ethnic minorities. EOP programs are found at most colleges and universities, and offer remedial courses, counseling, special financial-aid packages, and other types of support.

If you are physically challenged, you know how important it is to find an institution that is able and willing to meet your special needs. Personal visits and interviews will help you decide if the environment is physically and psychologically right for you.

Whatever your disability, you want a campus that is accessible and an academic curriculum you will be able to complete. You may need ramps, elevators, specially equipped restrooms, and drinking fountains. In addition, you may also want access to assistance in note taking, Braille texts, sign-language interpreters, or transportation programs. Of course, all these factors will play the same important role in your choice of occupation and career as in your choice of educational institution.

The All-Important Question: What about Money?

Getting an education can be very expensive. Whether you choose a private or a public college, you will be spending a lot of money. Moreover, time in school is time you might otherwise be earning, not spending, money. Yet the message is clear enough: Get as much education and training as possible. It will give you better preparation for the job market in the future. All this is fine, you may say, but how am I going to pay for it?

The good news is that a wide variety of options and sources of financial aid exists, depending on the type of institution in which you are enrolled and the type of aid for which you are eligible. The most common types of financial aid include grants, loans, scholarships, and tuition-payment plans from federal and state government programs, schools, foundations, and corporations.

These days, with the cost of a college education so high, most students need some type of financial aid package that combines grants, loans, and work-study. Grants are outright awards given strictly on the basis of need and do not need to be paid back. They include scholarships for people interested in specific areas; it is worth investigating these sources thoroughly.

The Guaranteed Student Loan Program (now known as the Stafford Loan Program) enables you to borrow from banks and other eligible lenders at low interest rates. Repayment generally begins after you finish your formal education, and allows you a number of years to completely repay the loan.

Federal work-study programs allow students who qualify on the basis of need to earn part of their educational expenses. The office at the school helps find jobs, and the employer pays a percentage of the hourly wage, with the federal government paying the remainder. Resources that provide specific information on financial aid options are listed at the end of this chapter.

The Bottom Line: College or Not?

Although this question is important to almost every teenager, there is no easy answer. A degree from a four-year college is certainly the first step in fields such as law, medicine, teaching, or engineering. In fact, quite a few additional years of postgraduate education are required in most of the professions.

However, you can also explore options *within* a given career, to see if there are tracks that require fewer years of preparation. For example, let's say you are interested in dentistry. If you don't want to go on for the many additional years of education required to be a dentist, you could choose to become a dental hygienist by getting a community college certificate. There are similar examples in many fields.

College is not for everyone. Reflect carefully before making that decision and the big commitment it requires. However, your career options will be broader if you are a college graduate, especially as the job market becomes increasingly more technical and specialized. The work world is so dynamic that one cannot predict today what jobs and careers will be important, or even around, tomorrow.

REFERENCES

Baumgardner, Steve. *College and Jobs: Conversations with Recent Graduates.* New York: Human Sciences Press, 1989.

Phifer, Paul. *College Majors & Careers: A Resource Guide for Effective Life Planning.* Garrett Park, MD: Garrett Park Press, 1987.

Renetzky, Alvin. *Career Employment Opportunities Directory.* 2d ed. Vol. 1: Liberal Arts and Social Sciences; Vol. 2: Business Administration; Vol. 3: Engineering and Computer Sciences; Vol 4: Sciences. Santa Monica, CA: Ready Reference Press, 1985.

Shields, Charles. *How To Help Your Teenager Find the Right Career.* Princeton, NJ: College Board, 1988.

Resources

for Finding Out about Career Preparation:
Going to College

Fiction

Klass, Sheila S. **The Bennington Stitch.** New York: Scribner's, 1985. 133p.

Amy's low SAT scores and high skill in cooking and sewing anger her mother. A high school English teacher, Amy's mother wants her to enroll at exclusive Bennington College. Amy's boyfriend has the same problem with the aspirations of his father, who wants him to become a doctor. This novel effectively illustrates the conflicting demands that parents sometimes place on teenagers.

LeGuin, Ursula K. **Very Far Away from Anywhere Else.** New York: MacMillan, 1976. 89p.

A strong and realistic story about two teenagers struggling with career aspirations and whether or not college is part of their future. Owen wants to become a scientist and to attend a fine private university, against his parents' wishes. Natalie wants to become an actress and also must make career and education decisions.

Nonfiction

BOOKS

Carter, Carol. **Majoring in the Rest of Your Life: Career Secrets for College Students.** New York: Farrar, Straus & Giroux, 1990. 212p.

This is an enormously useful book for every college-bound high school student. The author outlines how to achieve self-awareness; how to manage time for study, work, and a social life; how to obtain internships; and how to make the best use of study and travel experiences. Career-hunting tips are also included.

Dennis, Marguerite J. **Dollars for Scholars: Barrons's Complete College Financing Guide.** New York: Barron's Educational Series, 1989. 248p.

A fact-filled source book for parents and students that tells how, when, and where to apply for college scholarships. Also lists agencies where you will find financial grants, low-interest loans, and other practical sources of financial help.

Gelband, Scott, Catherine Kerbale, and Eric Schorr. **Your College Application.** New York: College Entrance Examination Board, 1986. 132p.

Written by a college admissions team and published by the College Entrance Examination Board, which administers the SAT and Advanced Placement exams, this book provides a good step-by-step introduction to all aspects of the college-application process.

Goldberg, Dick. **Careers without Reschooling: The Survival Guide to the Job Hunt for Liberal Arts Graduates.** New York: Continuum, 1986. 222p.

A comprehensive book that covers the concrete tools and practical information in any career search. The focus is on how the skills developed in the liberal arts are demanded by today's professional careers. Includes chapters by career-guidance experts as well as informational interviews with liberal arts graduates who are in fulfilling and diverse careers. This book will prove useful to teenagers interested in the liberal arts and wondering about their careers after college.

Hawes, Gene R. **Going to College While Working: Strategies for Success.** New York: College Entrance Examination Board, 1985. 142p.

Practical advice and tested strategies for fulfilling your college goals while employed. Suggestions are provided for locating and choosing the most suitable college and degree program. The book emphasizes different ways to finance your education and to succeed in college while holding down a job.

I Am Somebody. Alexandria, VA: Octamaroon Associates, 1988. 111p.

This guide to college selection, prepared by the staff of Octamaroon Associates, is especially designed for minority students, especially Hispanics and African-Americans, who may sometimes be the first in their families to consider college. A series of "false beliefs" (e.g., "I can't afford to go to college") are effectively addressed. Useful "nuts-and-bolts" sections cover such things as filling out college applications, applying for financial aid, and selecting the right school. This book is inspirational in tone and will be useful and encouraging for all readers.

Peterson's Annual Guide to Two-Year Colleges (787p.) and **Peterson's Annual Guide to Four-Year Colleges** (2739p.). Princeton, NJ: Peterson's Guides, 1991.

These guides, issued in a new edition each year, cover several thousand accredited U.S. two- and four-year institutions. Each guide contains college profiles, in-depth essays by admissions officers, and listings by majors and geographical areas. Peterson's also publishes guides to college admissions; study guides for college-entrance exams; and guides on scholarships and financial aid.

Pope, Loren. **Looking beyond the Ivy League: Finding the College That's Right for You.** New York: Penguin, 1990. 288p.

This book helps in the selection of the right college, and goes beyond the question on which some prospective students get bogged down: Does it have a good football record?

Sowell, Thomas. **Choosing a College.** New York: Harper & Row, 1989. 224p.

This book gets you started in the search for a college. You will learn how to find a college to fit your academic goals; the questions to ask about a school's curriculum; and other "future-saving" ideas.

Straughn, Charles, and Barbarasue Straughn. **Lovejoy's College Guide.** 19th ed. Englewood Cliffs, NJ: Monarch Press, 1989. 352p.

This completely updated edition provides comprehensive and authoritative information on all accredited American colleges—more than 2,500 two-year and four-year schools. It covers student body profiles, admission requirements, financial aid, study programs, campus life, and athletics.

Straughn, Charles, and Barbarasue Straughn. **Lovejoy's College Guide for the Learning Disabled.** 2d ed. Englewood Cliffs, NJ: Monarch Press, 1988. 192p.

This guide gives indispensable information on college programs available to students with a wide variety of disabilities.

ARTICLE

Larsen, Richard. **"Hopes, Opportunity—and State Lids."** *Seattle Times* (17 March 1991).

This article discusses how community college students view their futures, particularly their feelings about the value of and need for higher education. Although the setting is a single state (Washington), the issues raised are of general interest.

Nonprint Materials

Breaking Away
Type: VHS video
Length: 100 min.
Cost: Standard rental charge
Source: Regular video outlets
Date: 1979

This feature film is the story of four friends facing confusion about what to do following high school graduation.

College-Bound
Type: VHS video
Length: 5 videotapes, 85 min. each
Cost: Purchase $69 each; $315 set
Source: Guidance Associates
          Communications Park
          P.O. Box 3000
          Mt. Kisco, NY 10549-9989
          (800) 431-1242
Date: 1990

This series of five videos is packed with practical advice for the student in search of the right college. Titles are: Choosing the College That's Right for You, The Community College, Countdown to Acceptance, College Applications, and Making the Most of Your Campus Visit.

College Pressures
Type: VHS video
Length: 30 min.
Cost: Purchase $59.95
Source: PBS Video
          1320 Braddock Place
          Alexandria, VA 22314-1698
          (800) 424-7963
Date: Undated

Many high school students cite college-related pressures as a major cause of their drinking and drug abuse, dropping out, and depression. Planning for college can begin even before adolescence. Find out how teens learn to cope with their college decisions.

Organizations

American Association of Community and Junior Colleges
Suite 410
One Dupont Circle
Washington, DC 20036
(202) 293-7050
Dr. Dale Parnell, President

This association is a valuable clearinghouse that produces pamphlets, brochures, and other publications on individual colleges and on issues and concerns relating to community, technical, and junior colleges.

American Council on Education
One Dupont Circle NW
Washington, D.C. 20036
(202) 939-9300
Robert H. Atwell, President

The major advocate for higher education in the nation, this organization publishes an extensive set of materials relating to higher-education issues, colleges, universities, and educational organizations, including an annual fact book on higher education.

American Vocational Association
1410 King Street
Alexandria, VA 22314
(703) 683-3111
Dr. Charles H. Buzzell, Executive Director

This association provides information on the development and improvement of vocational, technical, and practical arts education. It publishes a semiannual job market update.

CHAPTER 6

Nontraditional Career Preparation

One of the most important things to figure out early in your career planning is whether you should go to college or go directly to work. Knowing how expensive a college education is, you may well think you cannot afford it and must begin earning money.

Interestingly enough, it may not be necessary for you to make an either-or choice between school and work. There are special programs that allow you to combine the two. Whether you work part-time, or alternate periods of full-time work and full-time study, these innovative and somewhat nontraditional approaches can help you afford a college education.

Career Testing in School: Experiential Education

The opportunity to include some type of on-the-job experience as part of your college education can be attractive. If you are like many other young people, you may still be somewhat unsure about what career or occupation will interest you after college. You may be a perfect candidate for enrolling in a field of study that includes an experiential education program. Although these programs have different names and vary according to the field and institution, they have in common an "experiential" quality: You enroll in a job program tied in with your academic studies. These off-campus work experiences allow you to earn academic credit and often a salary besides.

Cooperative Education

One well-known program is cooperative education, or "co-op" for short. Cooperative education programs are common in fields such as engineering, accounting, automotive technology, commercial art, retail management, computer science, drafting, and design work. They help students meet the steadily higher costs of attending a four-year college and obtain a college degree, which is an increasingly important credential in making you competitive in the twenty-first–century job market.

Most established co-op programs pay a salary for the work portion of the alternating work and study program. College tuition is sometimes paid by the employer, especially in many of the federal government's co-op programs and those of some large engineering companies. This can significantly reduce the costs of your college education. Enrolling in a co-op program may mean that it will take you longer to get your diploma—five years instead of four—but of course, you will get valuable on-the-job experience during that time.

Cooperative education allows you to enter jobs that relate closely to your studies and that the school considers part of your academic program. Choosing a career may be made a little easier if you can get some training and experience while you are still in school. Traditionally, college juniors have been in the highest demand for co-op positions, as companies have a year to look them over before graduation and possible hiring. But some companies try to identify talented students as early as senior year in high school.

Co-op students at major corporations are paid well, particularly in such fields as engineering, business, and science. Finally, remember that co-op experience not only looks good on your resume but also makes you more attractive in the job market. Employers often hire the cooperative education students who have been working for them when their studies are completed. Since most co-op placements are paid, you might think of this situation as an employer paying you while you test a career and complete your schooling at the same time.

Internships: Testing the Waters

Internship programs are found at all levels from high school to graduate school, but are most common during college. While some internships are paid, more often they are not.

What is an internship? In his book on the subject, Ronald Fry defines internships as part audition, part test, part question, and part answer. Intern programs may be part-time or full-time, during summers or during the school year. They give you a chance to "try on a career for size," that is, to test it for a limited time period so that you don't fear making a wrong choice. Internships provide a laboratory in which you can learn firsthand what a day-to-day job experience can be like. Both the intern and the employer benefit. The employer gets a needed job or service done at little or no cost; and you have the opportunity to test the waters, gain valuable experience to include on your resume, and decide if this is a field you really want to enter.

Students are often willing to volunteer their time in return for valuable on-the-job experience in a chosen career field. Interns interested in working for government agencies or non-profit organizations generally receive much lower salaries or no salary at all, although there are some grants to help supplement the low salary. Many internship programs focus on attracting young people from minority groups, particularly where employers want to diversify their work force. While not all internships lead to jobs after graduation, all provide valuable experience and an opportunity to be out in the "real world" while still in school.

Another aspect of experiential education that makes it so useful for career exploration is the opportunity it presents to discover whether you really need to get an advanced degree to work in a professional field. For instance, many rewarding health-care careers don't require you to go to medical school for an M.D. degree. By interning in a neighborhood clinic, you can see a full array of activities and jobs done by different kinds of health-care providers, many of whom are not doctors. You will be in a much better position to decide whether you need to pursue an advanced degree in health care.

Finally, participating in experiential education is especially useful if you are interested in working in "the helping professions." Volunteer work experiences are common in hospitals and clinics, schools, social service agencies, and rehabilitation facilities. They are all useful ways to acquire respected work credentials and to see if you would enjoy this type of work as a full-time career.

Experiential Education and the Physically Challenged

Internships and other types of experiential programs can be particularly helpful for the physically challenged student. The opportunity to gain work experience that fits your abilities will give you a head start in a competitive job market. Often, physically challenged students make an extra effort to upgrade their skills and knowledge, and these increased skills may more than balance out physical limitations. Many young people with disabilities impress future employers as highly motivated, dependable, conscientious, and productive workers.

Give Me a Break: Taking Time Off for Career Perspective

Some teenagers decide to take a break before continuing with school. Working for a few years may be a useful way to see what career opportunities exist and what specific skills and training they require. Some teens need to grow up a bit before heading off to college, and spending some time in the work force helps them do so.

By the way, the idea of taking time out is also becoming more common *after* college, as increasing numbers of new college graduates work for a few years before going on with more full-time education. Not only does a job help to pay the bills and to pay off student loans, but the added maturity often crystallizes your career interests. The average age for students entering graduate work in fields as different as law and social work, for example, is 31. Often the applicant has been working in the field in some capacity for several years, and has concluded that further education and more credentials are necessary for career advancement.

External-Degree Programs: On Your Own

There might be lots of reasons why full-time college is not in the cards for you right now. If so, you might want to explore the external-degree programs that allow you to learn at your own pace without attending traditional classes.

Correspondence courses from accredited colleges or universities are sometimes a useful way to build credits, especially if you live far from any educational institution. These credits will make your life easier if you eventually enroll in a traditional program. Correspondence courses, sometimes referred to as home-study or self-directed study, connect you with an institution that provides lesson materials. You mail assigned work to the school for correction, grading, and guidance, and corrected assignments are returned to you.

Courses for credit are offered through television and newspapers. Many feature audio and video cassettes that include tests and study materials and can be viewed at your convenience. Finally, increasing numbers of major companies, such as General Electric, Burroughs, and Aetna Life Insurance, offer excellent in-house training programs for employees at the work site.

Careers in the Military

Another career possibility for some people lies in the military services. You may be surprised to realize that the military, including all its branches, is the largest employer in the country. The military provides training opportunities and work specialities in a wide range of areas including professional, technical, clerical, construction trades, electrical, and mechanical occupations. All these occupations have civilian counterparts in the human-services, media, public-affairs, health-care, engineering, and various scientific fields.

Typically, those who enlist in the military do so for two to six years, though some choose to make the military a life-long career. While the military offers career opportunities, joining the armed services is a big decision and should not be taken lightly. Military life is more regimented than civilian life, and some people have trouble adapting to it. Dress and grooming requirements are strict and life is more formal; e.g., officers and enlisted personnel do not socialize together. Remember, once an enlistment contract is signed, there is no backing out and you are part of a military enterprise.

Major benefits of a military career include travel, free medical and dental care, and educational and vocational training, both during and after your period of service. However, the needs of the service branch always come first; and, of course, everything can change overnight during wartime.

If you are considering the military as a way to get career experience and learn an occupation, try to find out as much as possible about military life before you decide to enlist. Speak to friends and relatives with military experience. Determine what the military can offer you—and what it will expect in return. When you talk to a recruiter, ask him or her to assess your chances of being accepted for training in the occupation of your choice. Better still, take the ASVAB (Armed Services Vocational Aptitude Battery) offered at many high schools.

Apprenticeships: On-the-Job Education and Training

Apprenticeships are long-established programs that provide options for those who do not go to college or enroll for traditional higher education. As an apprentice you learn a skill in your chosen field by working under an experienced person. Apprenticeship programs typically last several years, and are common in such fields as cooking, bricklaying, plumbing, or auto repair. Generally you complete a probationary period and then sign a contract for a program that lasts from three to five years. By the end of this period, you might well be earning 90–95 percent of a journeyworker's wages, and be ready to receive a certificate indicating you are fully qualified for work in the field.

A two-year program on the art of building wooden boats in Maine provides a good illustration of a typical apprenticeship program. A small group of about 15 young people learn the trade of boat building by working under the watchful eyes of a master builder and assistant, by exchanging ideas with the other apprentices, and by practical experience.

This program, like many similar ones, requires a high degree of technical and manual skill and offers a combination of on-the-job training and related classroom instruction. In the classes, the instructors pull the theoretical and practical aspects of the job together.

Traditional or Nontraditional: What's Best for You?

We have tried to cover some of the many traditional and nontraditional educational options open to you after high school. Clearly, there are many ways to get career preparation, and each has advantages and disadvantages.

Let's take just one example: correspondence courses or external-degree programs. The advantages include: There is no need to attend classes; admissions requirements are flexible; there are no curriculum requirements; cost is low; students can work full-time. Disadvantages may be: there is no classroom contact with instructors and other students; it may be hard to maintain discipline and motivation; fully accredited programs are hard to find; and employers may not trust these degrees.

This is a good time to get out your career notebook, turn to a fresh page, and head it with "My Career in—" and "Educational Options." Note the educational requirements, not only for entry into the field but also for advancement. What educational options are available for your career? What are the advantages and disadvantages of these options?

Let's take one illustration: Suppose you have tentatively concluded that you would like to be a lawyer. Your research has indicated that you will most likely need to graduate from an accredited college or university, then attend law school, and, finally, pass the bar exam (the licensing examination in the state in which you want to practice law).

You have already seen that many options exist for your undergraduate degree (traditional four-year programs, two-year transfer programs from a community college, or some combination of classroom and independent study). Even in law school, there are options. Most law schools offer a traditional, three-year full-time program. This is highly intensive, requiring a great deal of study and preparation. It is hard to combine traditional law school with even a part-time job, except in the summer, although some students do it. But you could attend an evening law school while working at a full-time job during the day and obtain your degree in four or more years. Intensive bar-review courses after law school can help you prepare for the bar exam.

What are the advantages of a traditional versus a non-traditional route to becoming a lawyer? It probably will come as no surprise that if you attend a traditional four-year college or university it will be easier to get accepted at a three-year law school. You will complete the degree in a relatively short time and will make valuable contacts among your classmates, who will be your fellow lawyers some day.

On the other hand, the intensity and high pressure of traditional law school may not be for you. You might be better off taking things a bit more slowly and less intensely. An additional advantage is that, by working full-time, you will not be building up an immense financial debt. In the final analysis, you must weigh the pluses and minuses of the traditional, three-year, full-time law school experience. It will be a hard decision, but one that only you can make.

REFERENCES

"Careers in the Military." *America's Top 300 Jobs*. Indianapolis: JIST Works, 1990, 401–405.

Collison, Michelle. "Students Use Summer Internships To Gather Experience for Future Jobs." *The Chronicle for Higher Education* (26 July 1989): A-18, A-28.

Copa, George H. *Vocational Education and Youth Employment.* Columbus: National Center for Research in Vocational Education, Ohio State University, 1984.

Frederickson, Ronald H. *Career Information.* Englewood Cliffs, NJ: Prentice-Hall, 1982.

Gonchareff, Katya. "Internships: Testing the Waters." *The New York Times* (16 October 1983).

Resources

for Finding Out about Nontraditional Career Preparation

Fiction

Cross, Gillian. **Chartbreaker.** New York: Holiday House, 1987. 181p.

Janis May Finch is an angry 17-year-old student who wears a school uniform. But as Finch, she wears her karate outfit and sings with a rock group. Her career aspirations to get a job and work full-time with the band conflict with her mother's ideas for her. This novel illustrates someone struggling to enter a nontraditional career.

Naylor, Phyllis R. **The Year of the Gopher.** New York: MacMillan Atheneum, 1987. 224p.

This story takes place in Minnesota and is narrated by the hero, 17-year-old George Richards. High school readers will identify with this plucky hero who decides to defy parental wishes and not attend college. George's relationship with his parents, a lawyer and a teacher who expect him to attend a high-powered East Coast college, changes. George grows up, becomes genuinely confused about his future, but gains maturity and independence in the process. Anyone struggling with the big post–high school decisions and parental expectations will enjoy this story.

Werbsba, Barbara. **The Farewell Kid.** New York: Harper & Row, 1990. 155p.

Eighteen-year-old Heidi strikes out on her own, moves into an apartment, and opens her own business. The story deals with her struggles to maintain her independence and her business, and the self-discovery that goes along with both.

Nonfiction

BOOKS

Abrams, Kathleen S. **Guide to Careers without College.** New York: Franklin Watts, 1988. 110p.

This book discusses rewarding careers that do not require a college degree, in such fields as health care, sales and marketing, and the building trades.

Bennett, Robert L. **Career Planning Guide for Earning and Learning.** San Mateo, CA: Action Link Press, 1982. 60p.

Focused on ways students can use the cooperative education programs at many high schools and colleges to obtain paid, on-the-job experience. This book is helpful if you are thinking of combining school and work. It tells how to use part-time work, summer jobs, and volunteering in the nonprofit world to gain experience and career insights.

Bradley, Jeff. **A Young Person's Guide to Military Service.** Rev. ed. Boston: Harvard Common Press, 1987. 227p.

Even-handed and balanced advice concerning careers in the various branches of the military. Chapters on each of the services discuss specific offerings and note that those considering military service should think carefully about their options and their suitability for the military. The special situations of women and minorities are covered. Any young person considering the military should read this book.

Butterworth, Amy, and S. Migliore, eds. **National Directory of Internships.** Raleigh, NC: National Society for Internships and Experiential Education, 1989. 349p.

Complete descriptions of more than 26,000 internship opportunities across the country for students from high school through graduate school and beyond. The directory includes openings in government, nonprofit organizations, and corporate settings.

Cannon, Colleen, ed. **Internships: 16,000 on-the-Job Training Opportunities for All Types of Careers.** Cincinnati: Writer's Digest Books, 1983.

Includes information on internships and work-experience opportunities, sponsoring organizations, eligibility requirements, and application procedures.

Cohen, Marjorie. **Work, Study, Travel Abroad: The Whole World Handbook.** 10th ed. New York: St. Martin's Press, 1990. 496p.

This book introduces all the essentials of working, studying, and traveling abroad, and covers the map of available choices and options in 12 global regions on 6 continents. It also includes regional maps, country introductions, and recommendations of books and films.

Fry, Ronald W. **Internships.** Vol. 1. Hawthorne, NH: Career Press, 1988. 224p.

This is a useful guide to internship opportunities in advertising, marketing, public relations, and sales.

Gilbert, Sara D. **Lend a Hand: The How, Where and Why of Volunteering.** New York: Morrow, 1988. 160p.

A practical source book divided into three sections: why, where, and how to volunteer. It lists approximately 100 nonprofit organizations that offer volunteer opportunities, especially educational, religious, or youth-group settings.

Jobst, Katherine, ed. **1990 Internships: 38,000 on-the-Job Training Opportunities for All Types of Careers.** Cincinnati: Writer's Digest Books, 1990. 331p.

Each listing includes the duration or season of the position, pay rates, desired qualifications, duties and training, availability of college credit, and application procedures and deadlines. The book contains useful articles on career trends and quotations from interns.

Nivens, Beatryce. **Careers for Women without College Degrees.** New York: McGraw-Hill, 1988. 321p.

A useful guide for those people wanting to explore career fields for which a college education is not required. It covers many career areas, and includes training requirements, estimated salaries, and the outlook for the future. Designed as an employment guide for women, it also includes standard job-finding tips and much common sense advice.

Renetzky, Alvin, and Rebekah Berger. **Directory of Internships, Work Experience Programs and on-the-Job Training Opportunities.** 2d ed. 2 vols. Santa Monica, CA: Ready Reference Press, 1990. 660p.

A concise and up-to-date guide to the wide variety of internships and other hands-on opportunities currently being offered in both the public and private sectors. It also includes summer internships, work-study programs, and specialized opportunities for high school and undergraduate students. An invaluable guide to practical ways to gain career awareness and experience.

Roesch, Roberta. **You Can Make It without a College Degree.** Englewood Cliffs, NJ: Prentice-Hall, 1986. 230p.

Comprehensive source book detailing the many alternatives to careers that require college degrees. Included are tests, exercises, and worksheets to guide you in different directions.

Russo, JoAnn. **Careers without College.** Crozet, VA: Betterway, 1985. 160p.

Describes ten career fields in depth: advertising, banking, commercial art, data processing, fashion merchandising, finance, nursing, publishing, retail, and restaurant management and travel. The author covers everything of interest to people at the beginning of their careers.

Shanahan, William F. **College: Yes or No?** New York: ARCO, 1980. 304p.

Designed to help high school students who are choosing a career and deciding whether to attend college. This book is strongest in the area of careers open to people without years of college and postcollege education. It includes very comprehensive discussions of careers in the military and special government programs.

Ware, Cindy, ed. **Summer Options for Teenagers.** New York: Simon and Schuster, 1990. 576p.

An extensive and thorough catalog of programs for spending a productive summer in career testing and exploration. Information provided includes study abroad, outdoor adventure, classes and workshops, jobs, volunteer opportunities, sports programs, and performing-arts internships.

ARTICLE

Wallach, Ellen J., **"Charting Your Course: Live Career Skills."** In Joyce Mitchell, **See Me More Clearly.** New York: Harcourt Brace Jovanovich, 1980, 205–239.

Gives a thorough description of the types of career skills and opportunities that physically challenged young adults can develop, with a little careful research and planning.

Nonprint Materials

Soapbox with Tom Cottle: Working Teens
Type: VHS video
Length: 30 min.
Cost: Purchase $59.95
Source: PBS Video
           1320 Braddock Place
           Alexandria, VA 22314-1698
           (800) 424-7963
Date: 1985

The pressures and responsibilities of today's teenagers continually increase, particularly when they start to need money or begin a job. Listen to high school students discuss the importance of their jobs and the conflicts their jobs create with school, friends, and parents.

Working toward a Career

Type:	VHS video
Length:	12 min.
Cost:	Purchase $95
Source:	Career Aids
	Opportunities for Learning, Inc.
	Dept. XG 467
	P.O. Box 8103
	Mansfield, OH 44901-8103
	(800) 243-7116
Date:	1989

Programs that integrate work with academics such as work study, experiential education, and cooperative education are highly successful in preparing students for the work world. This video uses interviews with students, parents, employers, and successfully employed alumni to demonstrate the value of such programs.

Organizations

Association of Independent Colleges and Schools
One Dupont Circle NW
Washington, DC 20036
(202) 659-2460
Dr. James Phillipps, Executive Director and President

This association issues an annual directory of accredited institutions and also publishes a monthly newsletter on general issues related to higher education.

Bureau of Apprenticeship and Training
U.S. Department of Labor
601 D Street NW
Room 6100
Washington, DC 20212

See also the Apprentice Information Centers, operated by state employment services. The *Occupational Outlook Handbook* also covers apprenticeship programs.

Catalyst
250 Park Avenue South
New York, NY 10003
(212) 777-8900
Felice N. Schwartz, President

Catalyst, a national not-for-profit organization focusing on female concerns, offers many services, including a Career Resource Library and audiovisual centers. It publishes "Catalyst Career Opportunities" and a series of pamphlets called "Have You Considered . . . ?" focusing on specific careers. Other topics include choosing career options, starting a job hunt, and leadership opportunities for women.

The College Board
45 Columbus Avenue
New York, NY 10023
(212) 713-8000
Donald M. Stewart, President

Provides a variety of research and services to those making the transition from high school to college. This organization sponsors a variety of guidance, admissions, and placement examinations throughout the school year.

Council for Adult and Experimental Education
223 W. Jackson Boulevard
Suite 510
Chicago, IL 60606
(312) 922-5909
Pamela Tate, President

This association of colleges, universities, and organizations committed to adult and experimental learning publishes handbooks and guidebooks for faculty and students, and has developed a national network serving adult learners.

National Association of Trade and Technical Schools
2251 Wisconsin Avenue NW
Washington, DC 20007
(202) 333-1021
Stephen J. Blair, President

An association of private trade and technical schools that provide career education. This recognized accrediting agency publishes numerous career-focused handbooks and newsletters.

National Home Study Council
1601 18th Street NW
Washington, DC 20009
(202) 234-5100
William A. Fowles, Executive Director

This association publishes a directory of accredited home-study schools for those who are interested in learning more about correspondence courses.

National Society for Internships and Experiential Education
3509 Hawarth Drive
Raleigh, NC 27609
(919) 787-3263
Jane C. Kendall, Executive Director

This association publishes *Internships*, a helpful annual reference guide that contains more than 16,000 opportunities for short-term, training positions in many occupations.

CHAPTER 7

Practical Tips on Career Exploration

With Cheri M. Kaplan

By now you are well on the way to understanding yourself and your interests, skills, and values. We hope you are ready to put that information into action as you explore careers. In this chapter you will learn some practical guidelines for finding out about different professions, information on where to look for a job, tips on how to write a resume, techniques for interviewing, and suggestions on how to organize and manage your job search.

How do you find out more about a profession that interests you? Begin by reading all the literature you can find on your field of interest. There is a wide variety of sources you can explore: trade journals, directories, videotapes, company brochures, annual reports, newspapers, magazine articles, and job-hunting books. These will provide you with a foundation of knowledge.

The Informational Interview: Making Contact

Printed information is a place to begin to learn about a profession, but to get an "inside" look, you may want to talk to someone who is currently working in the field. This process is referred to as informational interviewing. The purpose of this interview is not to get a job, but rather *to collect information*.

Initially, you will need to identify contacts, that is, individuals who are currently working in a job or occupation in which you are interested. To gather a list of contacts you can ask family members and friends if they know anyone in the field. Teachers, principals, and counselors are also informative sources.

You may want to phone several organizations to establish some contact names. The personnel office of businesses in your field may assist you; however, do not speak only to the personnel or human resources department. Go directly to the source. Get the name of the person who is doing the job you think you might like to do.

After you have compiled a contact list, you are ready to approach the individuals and request informational interviews. There are several ways to do this; telephone calls and letters work best. When you speak with the individual tell that person that you want to learn more about his or her career because you are deciding about your own career direction. Next, ask to set up a convenient time for an informational interview, preferably lasting between a half hour and an hour.

Prior to the informational interview, *prepare.* You can do this by researching, formulating specific questions, and reviewing the interests, skills, and values that seem relevant to the career in question. The informational interview should be treated in a professional manner. First impressions are critical. Doing research on a career will allow you to present yourself as knowledgeable. For example, before interviewing an advertising coordinator, you should read about that occupation and about advertising in general.

After researching the career, you will be able to formulate specific questions. The following are some appropriate general questions you might ask in an informational interview. These are only suggestions. Be creative and develop your own questions.

What major responsibilities do you handle?

Can you describe a typical day?

What do you enjoy most about your job? Least?

What are the biggest challenges?

What are the usual entry-level positions in this field?

What is a typical career path?

What personal qualities should a person possess to be successful in this field?

What are the salary range and benefits package?

What trends do you see in the industry?

Whom else would you suggest I talk to?

Be sure to follow up the session with a thank-you note, no later than one week after the interview. You are probably keeping a career notebook; this would be a good time to write some notes in it about your impressions of the interview. In addition, you may find it helpful to start a card file of contact names that you can refer to later, during your job hunt.

The Job Hunt

Informational interviews help you to fine-tune your career interests. Once you have a focus you are ready to begin the job hunt. The job market has various levels of visibility. This means that many available jobs may never actually be advertised. There are many sources in which you can look for jobs:

PUBLISHED RESOURCES

Newspaper classified ads. Apply if you meet most, not all, of the qualifications.

Telephone directories

Magazines and journals

Company literature such as annual reports and internal newsletters

Specialized directories

Professional and trade magazines and newsletters

REFERRAL SERVICES

Government employment offices. Visit often; jobs get filled quickly.

School career centers

Employment agencies and search firms. Before signing, find out who pays the placement fee; it should be the hiring company, not you!

Job hotlines

Human resources or personnel office at the company

THE DIRECT APPROACH

Mail your resume and a cover letter. Be sure to send it to a specific individual. Call and ask the receptionist for the name of the manager of the department in which you are interested. *Do not send it "to whom it may concern."* Then, follow the correspondence with a phone call in a week to ten days.

Phone calls. Make cold calls, that is, call and ask if there is a job opening.

Job fairs, career days, open houses

Consider taking a volunteer or part-time position to "learn the ropes" and prove yourself as a responsible person.

PERSONAL CONTACTS (NETWORKING)

Family and relatives

Friends, classmates, and neighbors

Teachers and counselors

Church, synagogue, community organizations

It has been estimated that 80 to 90 percent of available jobs are never listed publicly. This phenomenon is referred to as the hidden job market. To tap into this market, it is important to develop your personal contacts, or network, and to approach companies in which you are interested, regardless of whether or not a job opening is listed.

Job hunting is difficult. Be persistent. After you send a resume and a cover letter, follow up. Make a call every other week or so to find out the status of your application.

Take a break from job hunting every once in a while and relax; call a friend, go to a movie, or do some physical exercise. Don't get discouraged; rejection is common, but you must persevere. An offer will come when there is a fit between you and a job position. Keep looking!

Show Yourself Off: The Resume

In order to be effective in your job search, you need to design a good resume. A resume is a brief summary of your skills, education, experience, personal qualifications, and activities. Often it is targeted to a particular career. Its purpose is to gain you a personal interview.

A resume should be focused and concise, usually no more than one or two pages; it should not be an all-inclusive recap of your entire life. It usually takes two to five drafts to perfect your resume. In addition you may need to develop several versions to target various job markets. The more targeted your resume is toward a specific position, the better.

Before you write your resume, take a personal inventory. Review your past education, work experience, activities, internships, volunteer work, strengths, and weaknesses. Begin with your most recent experiences and describe each of your key activities in detail. Include your responsibilities, highlight the skills you developed and the accomplishments you achieved. And be specific.

To put this information on a resume, select the information that is most relevant to the position you are seeking. A typical resume usually includes:

1. *Job objective:* This is an optional, concise statement of the position desired. Focus on your short-term objectives and stress what you can do for the employer. Alternatively, you may decide to elaborate on this statement in your cover letter.

2. *Experience:* Include job experience as well as volunteer and internship experience. If you are including more than paid work experience, you can title this section "leadership experience" or "project experience." The most recent information should be listed first.

3. *Education:* Include all degrees earned after your high school diploma. Be sure also to include summer courses, special seminars or programs of study, or any degree program in which you are currently enrolled.

4. *Activities, honors, and awards:* Extracurricular activities and community activities could be included in this section, especially ones that are relevant to the position or field.

5. *Qualifications or skills:* This is the place to list skills that support your candidacy for the position.

6. *Personal or interests:* Optional. This category allows some personality to be added to the resume. It is advisable to include only those things that seem relevant to your career goals or to a specific position; for example, language skills.

7. *References:* A brief statement indicating that references will be provided upon request. In addition, it is a good idea to have a list of references—people the employer can call to ask for information about you—typed on a separate page so the names are available when they are requested. Be sure to call the people whose names you provide, *in advance,* so they will not be surprised by the employer's call. This gives you the chance to tell them what the position is and why you would like a recommendation from them in particular.

The following are sample resumes. The two samples included are a reverse chronological resume and a functional resume, the two most popular styles. The chronological format is most frequently used; it is an arrangement of qualifications with the most recent listed first. The chronological resume is the most standard form and is recommended in most cases. However, for individuals with little or no work experience or for those who are changing careers, the functional resume may occasionally be appropriate. The functional resume is an arrangement of qualifications, by category, which highlights transferable skills. Notice that both resumes use active verbs and are written clearly and concisely.

COVER LETTERS

All resumes must be accompanied by a cover letter. The purpose of the cover letter is to introduce yourself. In addition it also serves to personalize and elaborate on your resume. Often, even more than the resume, it is strategic in getting an employer interested in you.

The cover letter must be typed and in a business format and should be addressed to a specific individual whenever possible. In the first paragraph state the reason for the letter. Include the position you are seeking and mention how you became aware of the position. In the middle paragraph refer to the enclosed resume, and highlight aspects that are particularly relevant to the position. Explain what you know about the organization and its needs, and show how your skills, experiences, and characteristics can help meet those needs. Be specific!

In the closing paragraph, thank the employer for his or her consideration and express your interest in an interview. Explain that you will call within two weeks to assure that your correspondence has been received. And make sure to follow up with a phone call.

Show Yourself Off: The Interview

The next step is the interview. Knowing how to interview and practicing interview techniques can increase your chances of getting hired. It may be helpful to practice your interview in front of a mirror or with a friend or relative. What do you look like? How do you sound? Would you hire yourself? The interviewer is trying to figure out why he or she should hire you. Some tips that may help you gain the interviewer's approval are:

James J. Smith
100 Oak Street
Manhattan Beach, California
213-555-1212

OBJECTIVE

Part-time entry-level position in sales or telemarketing.

EXPERIENCE

Sales Associate, Celluland, 1990–1991

Sold car phones to corporations and private users
Maintained daily tally of sales and transactions
Achieved weekly and monthly sales quotas

Library Clerk, Los Angeles Public Library, 1989–1990

Organized and maintained library books
Assisted individuals in locating information and resources
Advised members on library procedures

EDUCATION

B.S., Business Administration (Marketing Emphasis), May 1995 (expected)
California State University, Northridge

SKILLS

Proficient in WordStar, WordPerfect, MacWrite, and Microsoft Word
Fluent in Spanish

ACTIVITIES AND AFFILIATIONS

Captain, Glendale High School Varsity Basketball Team
Co-chair, Student Judiciary Board, California State University, Northridge,
1991–1992

References furnished upon request.

Reverse Chronological Resume

James J. Smith
100 Oak Street
Manhattan Beach, California
213-555-1212

OBJECTIVE

Part-time entry-level position in sales or telemarketing.

ACHIEVEMENTS

Communication Skills
- Interacted with customers and associates
- Prepared and delivered presentations on product lines
- Trained and informed customers on usage and maintenance of cellular phones
- Knowledge of computer languages and proficiency in word processing

Sales Skills
- Sold cellular phones to corporate and private users
- Made cold calls to accrue a large customer base
- Maintained daily tally of sales and transactions
- Achieved weekly and monthly sales quotas

Financial Skills
- Negotiated pricing and bid jobs
- Coordinated lines of credit with banking institutions
- Assisted in the development and management of annual budgets

Organizational Skills
- Organized and maintained records and files on clients
- Responsible for managing and updating library files and book stacks
- Arranged direct mailings and a 10,000-person contact list

Leadership Skills
- Oversaw a two-person staff and supervised their daily tasks
- Held leadership positions on varsity sports teams
- Elected co-chair of student judiciary board

EMPLOYMENT HISTORY

Sales Associate, Celluland, 1990–1991

Library Clerk, Los Angeles Public Library, 1989–1990

EDUCATION

B.S., Business Administration (Marketing Emphasis), May 1995 (expected)
California State University, Northridge

References furnished upon request

Functional Resume

Dress professionally.

Shake hands firmly.

Make eye contact.

Speak clearly and slowly.

Think before you speak!

Bring an extra resume.

Arrive about 15 minutes early.

Don't smoke or chew gum.

Be aware of your posture. Don't slouch.

Typically the interviewer will ask you questions about your goals, your strengths and weaknesses, how you deal with problems, and why you are interested in this job. Basically the interviewer is asking, "Why should I hire you?" Be prepared to give some good reasons. Review your skills before the interview and think about which are strongest.

Carefully consider all responses before you speak. It is all right to pause or ask for a question to be repeated for clarification. Start off by providing a general answer, then get more specific, and finally give some examples. For example, in response to a question regarding your strengths, you might respond, "I believe my strengths are my interpersonal and communication skills, that is, my ability to listen actively and effectively respond to others. I have been involved in many clubs at school where I was able to get things done because I understood and acted on others' suggestions and opinions." Toward the end of the interview there is often time for you to ask questions. Some typical questions you might ask are:

What types of people are successful in your company?

What are the greatest challenges for someone in this job?

How would I be evaluated and promoted?

Remember that you are also interviewing the company representative to decide if there is a good match between you and the organization. In closing, express your interest in the company and your possible role within it. After the interview, write a brief thank-you note and repeat your interest in the position.

Do not expect to get the first job for which you interview. Keep trying! Learn from each interview and improve.

Good luck!

REFERENCES

Como, Jay. *Career Choice and Job Search*. New York: Meridian, 1986.

Hopke, William, ed. *The Encyclopedia of Careers and Vocational Guidance*. Chicago: J.G. Ferguson, 1987.

Osipow, Samuel. *Theories of Career Development*. Englewood Cliffs, NJ: Prentice-Hall, 1983.

Rogers, Bob. *Secrets of the Hidden Job Market*. Crozet, VA: Betterway, 1986.

Toropov, Brandon, Carter Smith, and J. Michael Fiedler. *Job Bank Series*. Holbrook, MA: Bob Adams, 1987–1989.

Resources
for Finding Out about Practical Tips
on Career Exploration

Nonfiction

BOOKS

Beatty, Richard. **The Complete Job Search Book.** New York: Wiley, 1988. 244p.

Helps you to define your objectives, write a resume, network, and interview, and contains other tips for job hunters.

Beatty, Richard. **The Perfect Cover Letter.** New York: Wiley, 1989. 179p.

This book looks at all the elements of a cover letter. It will help you to perfect your own. In addition, it touches on the important aspects of resume writing.

Bloch, Deborah. **How To Have a Winning Job Interview.** Lincolnwood, IL: National Textbook, 1987. 130p.

A helpful guide that offers advice on interviewing. It will help you to polish your interviewing style.

Como, Jay. **Career Choice and Job Search.** New York: Meridian, 1986. 96p.

A resource guide and workbook to help you locate jobs and apply for them. Contains many interesting activities.

Good, C. Edward. **Does Your Resume Wear Blue Jeans?** High school ed. Charlottesville, VA: Blue Jeans Press, 1989. 165p.

A unique book written exclusively for high school students about resumes, finding jobs, and applying to college.

Gramling, L.G. **Blood, Sweat & Tears: Calculating Your Career Costs.** New York: Rosen, 1986. 130p.

A guide to getting the job you want, this book discusses setting goals and implementing them.

Jackson, Tom. **The Perfect Resume.** New York: Anchor, 1981. 208p.

This volume offers 55 samples of job-winning resumes. It also provides resume drafting forms and gives samples of resumes from various industries.

Lee, Rose. **A Real Job for You: An Employment Guide for Teens.** Crozet, VA: Betterway, 1985. 125p.

Concise guide for first-time job seekers. It covers each step of the job search: work permits, Social Security card, applications, interviews, and dressing right.

Marcus, John. **The Complete Job Interview Handbook.** 2d ed. New York: Harper & Row, 1988. 155p.

This handbook contains ways to get an interview and questions typically asked. It suggests ways to answer questions.

Medley, H. Anthony. **Sweaty Palms: The Neglected Art of Being Interviewed.** Rev. ed. Berkeley: Ten Speed Press, 1991. 190p.

A useful source to help you improve your interviewing techniques.

Parker, Yana. **The Resume Catalog: 200 Damn Good Examples.** Berkeley: Ten Speed Press, 1985. 314p.

Here are 200 excellent examples of resumes.

Perlmutter, Deborah. **How To Write a Winning Resume.** 2d ed. Lincolnwood, IL: National Textbook, 1989. 117p.

A step-by-step guide to writing a resume that captures the attention of the prospective employer.

Resume Writing: A Packet of Information. Washington, DC: Congressional Reference Service, Library of Congress, 1985.

Excerpts from diverse sources on ways to produce a well-written and distinctive resume. It includes a useful bibliography on job hunting and resume writing.

Yate, Martin J. **Knock 'Em Dead: With Great Answers to Tough Interview Questions.** Holbrook, MA: Bob Adams, 1991. 238p.

This book provides the best answers to some tough questions and discusses the best ways to answer questions in general.

Yate, Martin J. **Resumes That Knock 'Em Dead.** Holbrook, MA: Bob Adams, 1988. 214p.

Sample resumes to cover 150 different careers are presented. The book reviews the signs of a great resume.

ARTICLE

Burns, Robert. **"Marketing Yourself: The Art of the '90s Resume."** *Los Angeles Times* (9 September 1990): 18.

A useful article that provides key resume tips and suggests ways to target your employment biography for the industry and even the specific job you want.

Nonprint Materials

The Career Advantage Series
Type: VHS video
Length: 25 min. each

Cost: Purchase $400
Source: Cambridge Career Products
         One Players Club Drive
         Charleston, WV 25311
         (800) 468-4227
Date: 1989

Everything from resumes to interviews to keeping a job is detailed in this extensive series.

Career Exploration
Type: VHS video
Length: 15 min.
Cost: Purchase $60
Source: ESP Inc.
         1201 E. Johnson Avenue
         Jonesboro, AR 72401
Date: 1988

This video emphasizes the limitless opportunities for careers and defines many options. It includes steps of writing a resume, filling out an application, and preparing for an interview.

Career Exploration: A Job Seekers' Guide to the Outlook Handbook
Type: VHS video
Length: 21 min.
Cost: Purchase $79
Source: American Association for Vocational Instruction
            Material
         120 Driftmier Engineering Center
         Athens, GA 30602
Date: 1990

Discusses career tools people use during their career-exploration process.

Career Planning
Type: VHS video
Length: 16 min.

Cost: Rental $35; purchase $325
Source: Journal Films & Video
            930 Pitner Avenue
            Evanston, IL 60202
            (800) 323-5448
Date: 1990

This video involves the viewer in self-examination and presents challenges to using the imagination to consider a wide range of career possibilities.

How To Get a Job
Type: VHS video
Length: 60 min.
Cost: Purchase $119.95
Source: Cambridge Career Productions
            One Players Club Drive
            Charleston, WV 25311
            (800) 468-4227
Date: 1987

A good survey illustrating different ways to search for and land a job.

Your Future: Planning through Career Exploration
Type: VHS video
Length: 15 min.
Cost: Purchase $95
Source: Meridian Education Corporation
            236 E. Front Street
            Bloomington, IL 61701
Date: 1989

Designed for individual or classroom use, this video guides you in the assessment of career possibilities.

CHAPTER 8

Moving toward the Equal Opportunity Workplace

One of this book's themes has been that you will have a better chance of attaining your career goals if you thoughtfully look at your own talents, abilities, and interests; carefully assess the job market to gain a better understanding of where the job opportunities are today and tomorrow; and do all that is necessary to obtain the appropriate training and education.

If you take the time to do these things, it will make your path to career fulfillment easier. However, no matter how hard you work at it, the path to career success will not always be as rosy as this scenario might imply. Apart from the normal pitfalls and career setbacks any individual can expect to encounter at times throughout his or her working life, certain groups continue to face a work world that is sadly unequal in rights and opportunities.

As reluctant as we may be to admit it, job opportunities in our society still reflect ingrained stereotypes and prejudices. U.S. society has a long history of discrimination against women, ethnic and sexual minorities, the elderly, and the disabled. While things are better than they were just a few years ago, people in these groups still encounter hidden stumbling blocks.

As a teenager ready to take that first big step into the "real world" of jobs and careers, you are probably optimistic about your future and confident of your ability to overcome most obstacles. And so you should be. But you also should be aware of the realities of the job market and the subtle and not-so-subtle barriers you may encounter. The more you understand the prejudices of many people you will meet on the job, the better prepared you will be to overcome them.

Some Harsh Realities: Stereotypes and Discrimination

Manuel, age 17, has just graduated from high school, the first in his family to get that far. Unlike his parents who are both blue-collar workers, Manuel hopes to go on to college and major in business administration. He needs to work for a few years to earn money for college and is carefully planning his career strategies.

A job announcement for an entry-level position in a major downtown bank attracts his attention. Dressed neatly, he fills out the job application, careful not to make mistakes in grammar or spelling. His references include his high school principal and the minister of his church.

Manuel is never called for the interview.

Susan, age 23, has been working at the main office of the telephone company for the past four years. During that time, she attended community college at night to improve her skills in areas from accounting to writing. Her evaluations have always been excellent, and during the past year she was asked to serve as the trainer for the newly hired employees.

A supervisory position has just been posted and several of her co-workers urge her to apply for it. Her interview seems to go well, but she is dismayed when a young man she has trained receives the promotion.

Wanda, age 19, is very excited. She has applied for a position as a paralegal in a large downtown law firm and has been called in for the interview. She dresses carefully, remembering not to wear too much makeup or perfume, and practices her interview skills with her girlfriend, as the career books she has been reading have advised. She has done word processing in several law firms while getting her paralegal credentials, and is excited about making this important career move.

During the interview, she casually asks whether any provisions for child care are available to employees, as she has a preschool daughter whom she is raising by herself. Wanda receives a polite letter informing her that someone else was hired for the position.

"Wait a minute," you might say at this point. "These kinds of things may have happened to my parents, or even my older brother or sister. But this is the 1990s. Isn't that kind of job discrimination a thing of the past? And aren't women and minorities entering nontraditional professions like law, medicine, and engineering in record numbers?"

There has been great progress, of course. Today, women are welders, truck drivers, and legislators—once all-male fields. A woman justice sits on the U.S. Supreme Court, a large Texas city boasts a woman chief of police, and a major university, known for its football program, has hired its first woman athletic director. Asian-Americans, Hispanics, and African-Americans are moving into training programs and business careers where formerly there were only white faces, and some of the largest cities in the United States have African-American mayors. Federal and state laws require nondiscriminatory workplaces. Surely, job discrimination is becoming a relic of the past. Right?

Wrong! Look again. The picture is not as rosy as it seems at first glance. Prejudices against Spanish-surnamed persons, female single parents, homosexuals, or African-American men, for example, are deeply rooted, even though it has become both illegal and unfashionable to express these views. These prejudices emerge strongly when minorities and women are seen as moving into jobs that have been the exclusive province of white males, who may feel that their jobs are threatened and may join a backlash against these changes. Finally, many women and minorities have discovered that they can move only so far up the ladder before bumping their heads on an invisible ceiling.

You've Come a Long Way, Baby!

In 1966 the founders of the National Organization for Women (NOW) broke new ground with their vision of a true partnership between men and women based on equality in all aspects of life. More than 25 years later, how have we done?

Thanks to the hard work of the civil rights and women's movements, and the awareness and changes that gradually resulted, strong federal and state laws now prohibit sex and race discrimination in employment, education, credit, and housing.

Minorities and women have gained access to many occupations that had been closed to them. Civil rights laws enacted as early as the 1960s for minorities, and the 1970s for women, ensured federal guarantees of equal hiring and pay practices and policies. The good news is that discrimination against women and minorities is against the law. The bad news is that the labor force is still segregated, although less openly than in the past.

If you are female and about to enter the job market, you can expect to face the following realities, according to studies undertaken by the prestigious Hudson Institute:

> Two-thirds of you will probably work in one type of "women's work" or another, in positions such as secretaries, nurses, schoolteachers, and social workers. All these jobs have traditionally been poorly paid.

> No matter what your job or career, traditional or nontraditional, you probably will be paid significantly less than men doing identical or similar jobs. In 1988, according to the Bureau of Labor Statistics, women earned only 70 percent of what males doing work of comparable value made.

> You will undoubtedly have an easier time than your mothers and grandmothers did in gaining access to entry- and mid-level jobs, especially in fields where women were closed out in the past. But you will soon discover that most high-ranking positions are held by men, much as they always have been.

Minorities in the Workplace:
The Struggle Continues

Many whites believe that African-Americans, Hispanics, and other ethnic minorities have attained equal work opportunities. Unquestionably, as with sex discrimination, substantial progress has been made. Ethnic minorities are making inroads into previously off-limits jobs. Yet the realities of discrimination are still with us. If you are a member of an ethnic minority and about to enter the job force, you can expect the following realities:

> You are an African-American male planning to attend college and to graduate four years later. You can expect to earn only three-quarters of the salary of the white males who graduate with you.

> You are a Hispanic male thinking about going into factory work or another job in manufacturing. You learn quickly that there are fewer and fewer of these jobs around. And when the big industry layoffs occur, guess who gets laid off first?

> You are a Native American who has just completed high school, the first in your family to do so. Just when you thought you were getting ahead of the game, with lots of new jobs opening up, the rules change. Educational requirements keep increasing and one day you notice that you are falling further and further behind.

The Glass Ceiling

Those women and minorities who manage to overcome the age-old barriers of segregation and subtle discrimination and achieve a measure of career success often discover they can rise only so far up the career ladder. Indeed, no more than 1 or 2 percent of the top positions of power and prestige nationwide are filled by women or minorities.

More often than not, women and minority males bump their heads on what has been termed the glass ceiling. They are close enough to see the top, but an invisible ceiling stops them from getting there. A quick look at the gender and skin color of major business and political leaders shows how true this is. Minorities and women are getting their toes in the door, but they still have a long way to go.

Women have an additional problem if they plan to have families. You may well have to hold down two jobs, as your mothers and grandmothers have always done: your "outside" paid job and your "inside" unpaid job of caring for household and children. If you are a single parent, poor, and a woman of color, you are really up against it. Child care is so expensive and difficult to obtain that you may be effectively closed out of the most attractive jobs because you cannot pay for the help you need to care for your family.

Other Minorities

Job discrimination affects many other groups besides women and ethnic minorities. Sometimes it is harder to spot and even harder to fight.

Gay men and lesbians know about discrimination in most aspects of their lives. It comes as no surprise to them when an employer's biases translate into unfair hiring and promotion practices that may be difficult to prove, but are nonetheless real.

The physically challenged encounter discrimination in the job market, too. Citing the extra expense of installing special equipment or remodeling to make a workplace wheelchair-accessible, many employers simply find excuses not to hire someone with a physical disability.

Finally, thousands of older Americans experience age discrimination constantly, especially if job circumstances force them into a new occupation where the skills accumulated over a lifetime are no longer valued. Although research shows that older workers are steadier, more reliable, and have all their mental capacities intact, many employers are hard to persuade.

Where Does This Leave You?

The job picture for women and minorities is a complex one. Though many doors have opened that were previously tightly shut, discrimination and prejudice still linger. Many people feel that the government is not strict enough in enforcing the rules of fairness and equality.

You certainly need to give some thought to your career choices in light of these realities. Whether you are male or female; white, black, or brown; homosexual or heterosexual; disabled or able-bodied, your future career is yours to make—and no one else's. If you are strong-minded and courageous, you will be able to move forward in your occupational and career choices, even though it will not always be easy. The game is changing, and new rules are being made all the time.

Parents used to frown on little girls who wanted to play with trucks and little boys who wanted to play with dolls. Today, big girls who want to play football still have a hard time dealing with the attitudes of many parents, coaches, and other players. And big boys who want to take ballet lessons or learn to sew and weave still have a struggle on their hands as they go up against ingrained expectations of what boys and girls ought and ought not to do. And while it is true that men have always had a much wider range of career choices (after all, men could always choose to be elementary schoolteachers, but women could not always choose to be school principals), today both males and females have far more job opportunities from which to choose.

A Special Word about Math and Science

This is an appropriate place to point out the importance of getting good high school preparation in mathematics and science. It is true that you may be considering a job in the trades or technical fields that does not require a college degree. However, careers in word processing/data entry, laboratory technology, drafting, carpentry, and electronics, all *do* require math competence.

One theme that occurs often throughout this book is that you may well change your mind about possible fields of interest. Indeed, you are likely to make a number of different job and career choices throughout your life. Given the increasingly specialized job world, even if you are unsure just what career track will be right for you, it is a good idea to take at least three years of high school math, preferably four, while you are still in high school. You might be surprised to realize how many occupations, ranging from architecture to astronomy and forestry, require some high school preparation in mathematics. Particularly if you are a woman or minority hoping to enter a nontraditional field, the stronger the preparation you bring to it, the better.

Take Heart: You Need Not Be Alone

Despite the negative attitudes and prejudices that still exist, things are not that bleak. Certainly, the job market has begun to open up. And you will find people in it ready to lend a helping hand and to give you the benefit of their experience. Today women are building bridges, working as engineers, digging ditches, and pursuing careers as judges or bank managers. Hispanics and African-Americans are serving as lawyers, surgeons, and architects.

One thing you can do as you explore career ideas and begin to work is turn to women and minorities who may have preceded you for advice, moral support, and good counsel. Find someone to serve as a mentor, one who can show you the ropes and help you navigate the unknown waters of a new job.

How can you tell if someone is discriminating against you? Maybe your boss was just tense that day and everyone else felt his anger also. What about behavior that seems to be racial prejudice or sexual harassment? These things do occur, and if they do, you need to know what to do and whom to talk to about it. But it is also possible to misunderstand some behavior or take some legitimate criticism as a personal slur. Turning to someone you trust on the job can help you test your perceptions and provide you with support and guidance.

As you come to understand who you are, what you like to do, and how you want to spend your time, you are preparing to choose an occupation that best matches your goals. If you are determined, you can overcome the old stereotypes. You may sometimes encounter barriers along the way due to lingering negative or disapproving attitudes of co-workers, and occasionally even your own family and friends.

If you choose a nontraditional career route that has had few women or minorities, you may periodically wonder if it is all worth it. Being a trailblazer or pioneer is hard, and you may feel discouraged at times, especially if you are the token woman or minority in a stressful job situation. But think how much easier it will be for the next person, perhaps your own daughter or son, to follow in your footsteps. That may make it worthwhile.

There are no right and wrong choices. As long as you explore all the options open to you, no matter how unusual they seem to others, you will be in a better position to make the choices that are right for you. Just as you turned to those who preceded you for moral support and help, as you move up the ladder you will be able to show good will to the ones behind you. In this way, things will be easier for the next person who enters through the door you have helped to push open. Perhaps someday you will be in a position to extend a helping hand to someone else, down there peering up, looking for the crack in the glass ceiling.

REFERENCES

Barone, Michael. "The Inward Turn of Black America." *U.S. News and World Report* (8 May 1989): 32–33.

Cauley, Constance D. *Time for a Change: A Woman's Guide to Nontraditional Occupations.* Cambridge, MA: Technical Education Research Centers, 1981.

Gerson, Kathleen. *Hard Choices: How Women Decide about Work, Career, and Motherhood.* Berkeley: University of California Press, 1985.

Hudson Institute. *Opportunity 2000: Creative Affirmative Action Strategies for a Changing Workforce.* Washington, DC: Hudson Institute, 1988.

Iglitzin, Lynne, and Ruth Ross. *Women in the World: 1976–1986, A Decade of Change.* Santa Barbara: ABC-CLIO, 1986.

Michelozzi, Betty. *Coming Alive from Nine to Five.* 3d ed. Mountain View, CA: Mayfield Press, 1988.

Morrison, Ann M., et al. *Breaking the Glass Ceiling.* New York: Addison-Wesley, 1987.

National Research Council, Committee on Women's Employment. *Computer Chips and Paper Clips: Technology and Women's Employment*. Washington, DC: National Academy Press, 1986.

Rix, Sarah E., ed. *The American Woman, 1990–91: A Status Report.* New York: W.W. Norton, 1990.

Williams, Christine. *Gender Differences at Work: Women and Men in Nontraditional Occupations*. Berkeley: University of California Press, 1989.

Resources

for Finding Out about Equal Rights in the Workplace

Fiction

Clarke, Arthur C., and Gentry Lee. **Cradle.** New York: Warner Books, 1988. 293p.

Photojournalist Carol Dawson charters a fishing boat off the Florida coast, ostensibly to study whales but in reality to check on the U.S. Navy's search for missing test missiles. She and her companion diver find a huge underwater chamber filled with advanced technological devices planted there by alien robots. A lively tale showing a female heroine in a decidedly untraditional occupation.

French, Michael. **The Throwing Season.** New York: Dell, 1980. 216p.

Henry, a Native American high school student who has heard his father talk often about the prejudices and discrimination against Indians, is determined to succeed. His goal is to excel at shot-putting, and his adventures to succeed in the sport make an exciting story.

Gregorich, Barbara. **She's on First.** Chicago: Contemporary, 1987. 288p.

A baseball scout follows the growth and development of talented Linda Sunshine from Little League through college. She has all the talents and skills she needs, but encounters prejudices of fans and players when she signs with a major league team. Finally, through ability and courage, she overcomes these prejudices and is able to play the game she loves.

Johnson, LouAnne. **Making Waves: A Woman in This Man's Navy.** New York: St. Martin's Press, 1986. 70p.

LouAnne decides on a career in the U.S. Navy and learns to fight for what she wants, to meet challenges head on, and to win. She learns she has to be twice as good as the men to get half their rewards. Military careers and women are still somewhat incompatible, as this book illustrates.

Knudson, R.R. **Zan Hagen's Marathon.** New York: Signet, 1985. 156p.

Zan Hagen wins a three-mile running championship with five-minute miles and is convinced that moving to the Olympics is a marathon away. Her coaching, practice, and training experiences affect her values and cause her to question whether winning is everything. A good story about a woman in competetive athletics and her own personal growth.

Ronyoung, Kim. **Clay Walls.** Seattle: University of Washington Press, 1987. 301p.

This is the story of Haesu, a Korean woman who came to the United States in 1905, reluctantly following her fiancé who had fled Korea. Life in California proves less than ideal, and the blatant discrimination against Asians looking for jobs and housing is well described. Despite the cultural differences and societal pressures, Haesu manages to raise her family and instill a sense of their heritage. This book gives a moving portrait of discrimination against an ethnic group and their struggles in many areas, including employment.

Nonfiction

BOOKS

Allen, Maury. **Jackie Robinson: A Life Remembered.** New York: Franklin Watts, 1987. 260p.

As the first black man to play major league baseball, Jackie Robinson was attacked verbally and physically when he began his career with the Brooklyn Dodgers in 1947. His courage, intensity, ability, and influence on others are recalled here by family, friends, and fellow players.

Beisser, Arnold. **Flying without Wings: Personal Reflections on Being Disabled.** New York: Doubleday, 1989. 189p.

Dr. Beisser, a successful psychiatrist who is also a paraplegic, provides important insights into the world of loss and disability. He also discusses the ways in which the sports-obsessed American culture has made us think of ourselves as winners or losers.

Benoit, Joan. **Running Tide.** New York: Knopf, 1987. 213p.

Joan Benoit was born with a competitive spirit and a sense of adventure that helped her become one of the premier runners of our time. Her autobiography describes her growing up, her dreams of becoming a great skier, and how she turned to running instead after a leg injury. This story illustrates the discipline and perseverance needed for a competitive sports career.

Brown, James. **James Brown: The Godfather of Soul.** New York: Thunder's Mouth, 1986. 352p.

James Brown's music has had an enormous impact on soul, rock, and rap music. Brown tells about his birth in a rural shack, his childhood living in a house of prostitution, his prison sentence for robbery, and his rise to fame and fortune. The reader will get a sense of the intense racism a black man in the United States must face every day of his life.

Gordon, Alison. **Foul Ball! Five Years in the American League.** New York: Dodd Mead, 1985. 204p.

As one of the first female reporters to cover professional baseball, Alison Gordon had difficulty in getting locker-room interviews, being accepted as an equal by her fellow sportswriters, and being treated fairly by baseball management. Her account vividly illustrates the hardships and joys experienced by a woman in a nontraditional profession.

Levin, Beatrice. **Women and Medicine: Pioneers Meeting the Challenge!** Lincoln, NE: Media Publishing, 1988. 267p.

This book features the lives of women who have pioneered in the field of medicine, overcoming obstacles, barriers, and cultural attitudes that kept medicine a male-only field for so long. Covering the riots in medical schools when women tried to enroll, and women who achieved brilliant careers and Nobel Prizes, this book will certainly inspire everyone, particularly women contemplating this field.

Markham, Beryl. **West with the Night.** San Francisco: North Point, 1983. 320p.

An extraordinary autobiography of a woman who pioneered in two nontraditional fields, the training and breeding of racehorses, and aviation. In the 1930s, Markham became the first person to fly solo across the Atlantic Ocean from east to west. Her personal story of growing up in Africa and of her determination to break all molds and follow her own goals is inspiring and delightful to read.

Matthews, Jay. **Escalante: The Best Teacher in America.** New York: Henry Holt, 1988. 322p.

This remarkable Hispanic high school teacher inspired his underprivileged and Latino students to set standards in mathematics all but unequalled in secondary education.

Michelson, Maureen R. **Women and Work: Photographs and Personal Writings.** 2d ed. Pasadena, CA: New Sage, 1988. 178p.

Women in traditional and nontraditional jobs—firefighter, ironworker, waitress, bartender, physician, nurse, jockey—reveal their hopes, dreams, frustrations, and concerns in a portrait based on personal writings and photographs of today's working women.

Morrison, Ann M., et al. **Breaking the Glass Ceiling.** New York: Addison-Wesley, 1987. 229p.

A practical discussion of the barriers women encounter as they try to advance in the corporate world. Written clearly and without jargon, it includes interviews with women who have succeeded and their accounts of how they managed to advance their careers despite obstacles.

Mowatt, Farley. **Woman in the Mists.** New York: Warner Books, 1987. 400p.

This true story of ethnologist Dian Fossey and the mountain gorillas of Africa gives a vivid and fascinating portrait. Fossey, trained as an anthropologist, dedicated her life to trying to preserve an endangered species in the wilds of Africa. The story shows how a great obsession can be a lifelong career motivation. It should dispel any thoughts that women are too weak or frail to take on dangerous or unusual careers.

Sullivan, Tom, and Derek Gill. **If You Could See What I Hear.** New York: Harper & Row, 1975. 184p.

A moving autobiography of a gifted young man who became blind shortly after birth. Sullivan refused to accept the limits of his handicap and developed all his natural talents and abilities. He became a champion wrestler in school, a high academic achiever, a sportsman, a composer of popular songs, and a husband and father. The book is an inspiration to all young people, whether they have disabilities or not.

Wright, Bruce. **Black Robes, White Justice.** New York: Lyle Stuart, 1987. 214p.

The author, a judge on the New York Supreme Court, focuses on the great social distance between blacks and whites as they are judged in the courts, especially when street crimes are involved. The book is filled with anecdotes, many from his own youth marked with racial incidents and from his experiences as a judge. As harsh and disturbing as this book is, it is valuable for those interested in racism in the criminal justice area. It also makes vivid reading for anyone thinking of a law-related career.

ARTICLES

"Short-Changing Girls, Shortchanging America." *Report of the American Association of University Women.* Washington, DC: AAUW, January, 1991. 17p.

Presents the results of a nationwide poll on self-esteem, educational experiences, interest in math and science, and career aspirations of adolescents. The results show a striking decrease in self-esteem in girls, especially Hispanics, as they move through the high school years. Girls feel less confident about their abilities and less sure about their career aspirations.

"Women: The Road Ahead." *Time* (Fall 1990): 50–54.

This entire special issue of *Time* makes useful reading on the variety of issues facing women on the road to equality. Especially pertinent is the "On the Job" section discussing the twenty-first–century work force.

"Why Take More Math?" Seattle, WA: University of Washington Equal Employment and Affirmative Action Office, 1989.

A useful three-page pamphlet that emphasizes the importance of high school preparation in math and science, whether one is planning on going on to college and a professional career or into the trades or technical fields.

Nonprint Materials

Gorillas in the Mist
Type: VHS video
Length: 129 min.
Cost: Standard rental charge
Source: Regular video outlets
Date: 1987

The true story of famed ethnologist and anthropologist Dian Fossey, this feature film presents her struggles to carve out a nontraditional career working with mountain gorillas in the wilderness of Africa.

Hollywood Shuffle
Type: VHS video
Length: 82 min.
Cost: Standard rental charge
Source: Regular video outlets

Date: 1987

A feature comedy about racial stereotyping in the movie industry.

Nine to Five
Type: VHS video
Length: 111 min.
Cost: Standard rental charge
Source: Regular video outlets
Date: 1980

A feature film comedy about three bright secretaries frustrated by their foolish boss.

Voices from the Well
Type: 1/2" VHS video; U-Matic
Length: 45 min.
Cost: Rental $45; purchase $125
Source: Instructional Development Center
           University of California
           Santa Barbara, CA 93106
           (805) 893-3518
Date: 1984

Dramatic portrayals of extraordinary women from history, literature, and the arts. Includes Georgia O'Keeffe, Mary Harris Jones, Virginia Woolf, Gertrude Stein, Harriet Ross Tubman, George Sand, Saradi Devi, Caroline Herschel, Aphra Behn, and Guinevere.

Organization

American Association of University Women
1111 Sixteenth Street NW
Washington, DC 20036
(202) 785-7700
Anne Bryant, Executive Director

A century-old organization that promotes education and equity for women and girls. It provides funds for fellowships, research, and community action to raise awareness about issues that affect women, their families, and their careers.

CHAPTER 9

Summing It Up

No matter what type of job or career you eventually enter, one thing is certain. The work world will be a different place in the twenty-first century than it used to be. And the differences go beyond computers and robots. They have to do with quality of life and with new expectations today's workers bring to their jobs: that their home and family needs will be taken into consideration by their employers.

In the old days, all the job expectations were held by the employer. A new employee was expected to carry out the duties and responsibilities of the job description and to fit his or her schedule around the demands of the employer. Today, things are different. Whether it is because of the growing number of women entering the work force, the families that need two careers for economic survival, single parents, or all of the above, people want more time with their families and they expect their work lives to make room for this. The days when workers had to make either-or choices between their jobs and their families are gradually ending.

The Juggling Act: Everybody's Doin' It

It has never been easy to achieve a balance between the demands of work and the demands of family and personal life. Too often in the past the worlds of work and family competed with one another. Now, more employees are finding it increasingly difficult to separate their home lives from their working lives. After all, workers are also family members, and many have major family responsibilities.

In the past, women workers with young children could often turn to other female family members for help with child care. Today, these aunts and grandmothers are probably part of the work force themselves. Moreover, as parents and grandparents live longer and become frail and elderly, more employees, both women and men, are searching for extra hours in the day to provide care for both the old and the young members of their families.

When it comes time for you to enter your chosen occupation, you may find that personal factors are important to you. Perhaps you will be thinking of getting married and starting a family. Maybe you will be caring for a young brother or sister or an elderly or sick parent. Or you may simply feel that having quality personal time is important—time to engage in sports, to go dancing or to concerts, to go camping or hiking, or just to relax and have fun.

Responsibilities that were once viewed as only the woman's, such as care of home and children, are now often shared between the sexes. If you are a man, you may well be a more involved parent than your father and grandfathers were. And you may be troubled and guilty if you do not have enough time to spend with your children. Today some men sacrifice promotions, pay raises, and job status for the sake of their families.

Once, men were the breadwinners and their wives took care of the kids. It is different today and these differences will continue tomorrow. Wives work because one income is not enough, and more husbands are taking on a share of parenting and homemaking duties. As Dr. Joyce Brothers has noted, "For the first time in 10,000 years, males on all economic levels are putting their families over their careers." Maybe, as a father, you will one day assert your rights to be home to enjoy and help with your family, even if it means hard choices between family and career advancement.

Differences in families also affect job expectations and roles. The number of single-parent families, most but not all headed by women, is increasing. Should you be a single parent someday, supporting your family through your work and bearing all the responsibility for child rearing or perhaps caring for an elderly parent, you will realize how difficult these demands can be to meet alone.

These dilemmas are old news for women, of course, since women have always balanced job and family. In fact, women have long juggled their inside and outside jobs with precious little support along the way. By and large, this is still the case. Even as child care centers are built and employers extend parental leaves, most people still see women as having the main responsibility for home and children. However, as we look to the future, it seems clear that both women and men will expect their jobs to allow them the time, energy, and resources necessary to do a good job in their families as well as in their place of employment.

Moving toward a Responsive Workplace

It is encouraging to conclude a book on career exploration by noting that, as the twenty-first century fast approaches, the workplace is slowly but gradually becoming more responsive to individual and family needs. Topics such as pregnancy, maternity and paternity leaves, and the child care needs of working parents increasingly appear on the agendas of major companies, business conferences, labor unions, and the makers of laws and public policies.

These changes reflect the dramatic differences in the work force. Old assumptions that most employees were men whose wives stayed home and took care of children are long out-of-date. Today, the workplace is as diverse as you can imagine: two-earner couples, young single adults, childless couples, single women and men who are heads of families. There are workers with babies, workers with adolescent children, and workers who are caring for their aged parents. Not surprisingly, employers are finding that they have to be creative in designing benefits and employment policies to fit the needs of all these people.

How do you fit into all this? You are poised to enter the first stage of career exploration and preparation. You are making major decisions about occupations, careers, and traditional or nontraditional routes for training. It may seem remote, indeed, to think about the workplace conditions that will best fit your needs five and ten years down the road.

However, considering your personal and family needs and expectations in your career-search process is not only appropriate but vital. It is important to think about a vocation that will be responsive to these needs, whether you want to pursue leisure-time activity or spend "quality time" with your family. The time to think about these things is now, before you have embarked on a path that will be harder to change as your life gets fuller and more complex.

What Does This Mean for You?

Put most simply, when you consider a prospective career or occupation, try to look beyond such things as salary and job title. Even if you do not plan to start a family immediately, you may still want to find a family-friendly work setting.

Try to imagine how important you think it might be to have a flexible work schedule. Maybe you would like some early morning hours to allow for child care or even to make your commute easier. Increasingly, more jobs are allowing people to work out of their homes. Freelance writers, stockbrokers, telephone marketers, and computer programmers are examples of people who often have their offices in their homes. This makes balancing work and home responsibilities much easier, of course. If this balance seems important to you, consider an occupation where this kind of flexibility is permitted and encouraged.

Try to investigate the leave and benefits policies in the occupation you are considering. Are there provisions for paternal as well as maternal leave? You most likely will be a working parent, and you may want to find a workplace where leaves of absence are extended to either parent. And what about child care? Affordable and high-quality child care is fast becoming one of the most important fringe benefits a prospective employer offers.

As you think about these factors within the framework of your career choices, focus on the practical implications. If you plan to have children, the question of when you would start your family is a factor. Juggling pregnancy, child rearing, and child care with job demands is no easy task. It is even more difficult if you are still in school, in a job-training program, or in the entry phase of your career. You may wish to delay having children until you are farther up the career ladder.

There is no guarantee that the juggling act will ever be easy, of course, particularly for working mothers. But the farther along you are on your career track, the easier it ought to be. For instance, you may be in a better position to take an extended period off from work during the first year or two of a new baby's life. You may choose to shift from full-time to part-time work. If your employer has such options, you may be able to take advantage of job-sharing, flex-time, and other benefits designed to help working parents.

Of course, there are tradeoffs with everything. Will your boss consider you less committed if you ask for six months off? Will your co-workers take you less seriously if you work half-time for a while? Will you jeopardize your advancement and raises? Will reentry be hard if you are out of your field for a period of time? There are no easy answers to any of these questions, but they are all things you will need to think about.

The question of child care has important practical concerns as well. At some point you probably will be faced with hard questions and choices about family issues. Not only will you have to look at the cost and availability of child care, but you may have to weigh the advantages and disadvantages of having a child-care worker in your home against putting your child in a group facility.

You don't have to wrestle with these family issues and others all by yourself. Many employers, especially large firms, have employee-assistance programs (EAP) or the equivalent. These programs have staff members whose job is to help employees deal with personal and family problems. Of course, you have to take the initiative to seek out these services. Increasingly, EAPs provide counseling, information, and referral services on everything from alcohol and drug problems, to child care services, elderly family members, and job-related stress. If you feel overwhelmed, be sure to check on these services and don't try to tough it out by yourself.

Meshing Work and Leisure

There may be some controversy about what exactly the twenty-first century workplace will look like, but on one thing almost everyone agrees: There is already a shift away from the patterns our parents and grandparents knew. Already, in the mid-1990s, more people are becoming entrepreneurs, that is, starting their own businesses. More people are exploring work-at-home options. And more workers expect that their work and leisure-time activities will mesh, rather than conflict or compete.

The old adage, "All work and no play makes Jack a dull boy," has never been more appropriate. Leisure-time activities open to high schoolers, college students, and adults serve to build skills and knowledge and even lead to occupations. In his book, *The Changing Workplace,* Carl McDaniels includes an extensive list of leisure activities and related occupations in both part-time or full-time work. As he points out, a dancer may operate a dance studio, a musician might manage a symphony orchestra, or an actor could end up running a summer theater. Similarly, skill and knowledge acquired playing tennis may lead directly to a career operating a sporting-goods shop, teaching tennis, or marketing for a sporting-goods manufacturer.

Other leisure activities are followed throughout life but never lead to an occupation. They can provide a full range of satisfactions that have nothing to do with how one earns a living. Many people obtain a great deal of satisfaction and pleasure from being amateurs in various cultural, sports, social, or leisure activities, and this is important too. As you consider the type of career or occupation you wish to explore, you may wish to choose a field that provides you the flexibility and time to pursue these outside activities.

Myths and Realities: The Career Test To End All Tests

If you have gone through this book carefully, you should have a pretty good idea of the realities of choosing a career. In fact, you will probably have better knowledge than a lot of people who will try to give you advice. Although these people mean well, you will do better to listen to your own instincts and trust your good sense. You will be surprised to realize that you are smarter than you think you are, certainly about the one person most important to you: yourself.

To prove this point, here is one last test. It sums up many of the themes of earlier chapters. The false answers represent the myths and the true answers the realities of the world of work and career planning. Let's see how well you've learned the difference.

TRUE OR FALSE?

1. What you study in high school has little or nothing to do with your future career. FALSE!

   As we stressed in Chapter 1, high school teaches you the skills of reading, writing, computing, logical thinking, and analyzing, all of which are essential in the simplest as well as the most difficult of jobs. Learning good work habits in high school will help you throughout your work life. Don't put high school down!

2. The only way to get a good job is to go to college. FALSE!

   As we discussed in Chapters 5 and 6, college is not your only option, nor is it a guarantee to a high-powered career. While certain careers such as the professions require college and postgraduate degrees, many others draw people who have had different kinds of experience and training. In general, the more education you get the better, of course, but be sure it is the right kind and that you're doing it for the right reasons, that is, right for you and your goals.

3. Sexism and racism are things of the past. FALSE!

   As we discussed at length in Chapter 8, things are getting better, and fewer doors are closed to women and minorities than in the past. But these changes are still incomplete. Be wary of the myth that there is full equality in the job market, no matter what your skin color or gender.

Women and minorities are still clustered in certain occupations and still bump heads on the glass ceiling of career advancement. Do not be discouraged, but be alert to these realities. You should also recognize that not all criticism or setbacks you encounter can be laid at the foot of discrimination. Try to be objective and test out your perceptions with a co-worker or someone you trust before you jump too quickly to charge discrimination.

4. Everyone works a 9–5 day and a 40-hour week. FALSE!

As we have noted, the work world is changing rapidly, and increasingly there is no typical workday. Men and women now often choose to work part-time, take jobs with flexible hours, or seek jobs that allow them to work out of their homes.

A Few Parting Words

We have been talking about myths and realities, and this seems a good time to put to rest one important myth that has not yet been addressed: the idea that there is *one right job* out there for you, and that you will not be happy until you find it. This is like the old belief on which boys and girls used to be raised, that there is only one mate for you, and when you find him or her, you will live happily ever after! Both these false beliefs should be put to rest forever.

It is true that in the past, many people entered an occupation and remained in it throughout their working lives. Whether they were happy or bored, they never considered the possibility that they could retrain and change jobs. Today, if a job becomes boring and unsatisfying, it is common for workers to move on to something else and not be considered a failure. Especially in a job market that changes rapidly all the time, you need to be open to the possibility of retraining and getting additional education, not once but perhaps several times in your life.

It may seem strange to be talking about learning new skills and changing careers now. After all, you are just on the verge of making your very first career move. How can you possibly contemplate doing something different when you have not even begun the first thing? Yet if you think about all the people who have changed careers many times, ordinary folks as well as famous people, and realize how long your working life will be, you will not find the notion of job shifts and changes so peculiar.

One last point needs to be emphasized over and over again: There is no right and wrong when it comes to career choices and decisions. Choosing a career is not like solving a math problem. There is no one right answer. Rather, career planning needs to occur throughout your lifetime, and you can expect it to take many different forms depending on where you are in your life. None of these career decisions is forever and there is nothing wrong with people who decide that they would be happier doing something else. We all make the best decisions we can with the information and options available at a given time. If more information comes along or new opportunities open up, try to prepare yourself to seize the chance and move on.

The process of career choice and decision making should be exciting. Armed with self-knowledge and understanding about who you are and where you want to go, and with sufficient information and resources, you are on your way.

REFERENCES

Brothers, Joyce. "The New Man in the House." *Los Angeles Times* (12 August 1990), E-1, E-8.

Child Care: A Workforce Issue. A Report of the Secretary's Task Force. Washington, DC: U.S. Department of Labor, 1988.

Kammerman, Sheila B., and Alfred J. Kahn. *The Responsive Workplace: Employers and a Changing Labor Force*. New York: Columbia University Press, 1987.

McDaniels, Carl. *The Changing Workplace*. San Francisco: Jossey-Bass, 1989.

Meier, Gretl S. *Job Sharing*. Kalamazoo, MI: Upjohn Institute for Employment Research, 1979.

Index

Lynne B. Iglitzin is Assistant Director of the Institute for Public Policy and Management at the Graduate School of Public Affairs at the University of Washington in Seattle. An author of books and articles in a variety if topics, Dr. Iglitzin has a Ph.D. in Political Science and has taught at the University, community college, and secondary school levels. For ten years she directed a career-testing internship and field experience program at the University of Washington. Dr. Iglitzin has personal experience with career exploration and change, having worked in academic, nonprofit management, and policy researching settings. She has raised three children and has experienced firsthand the challenge of juggling career and family.